MARTHE JOCELYN

A Home for Foundlings

A LORD MUSEUM BOOK

D1279468

Tundra Books

Museum Edition

Published in Canada by Tundra Books,
481 University Avenue, Toronto, Ontario M5G 2E9

Published in the United States by Tundra Books of Northern New York,
P.O. Box 1030, Plattsburgh, New York 12901

Library of Congress Control Number: 2004110124

Library and Archives Canada Cataloguing in Publication

Jocelyn, Marthe
    A home for foundlings / Marthe Jocelyn.

Published in cooperation with Foundling Museum and LORD
    Cultural Resources Planning and Management.
Includes bibliographical references and index.
ISBN 0-88776-709-5

    1. Foundling Hospital (London, England) I. Lord Cultural Resources
Planning and Management Inc. II. Foundling Museum III. Title.

HV847.G72L65 2005   362.73'2   C2004-904140-1

We acknowledge the financial support of the Government of Canada through the Book
Publishing Industry Development Program (BPIDP) and that of the Government of Ontario
through the Ontario Media Development Corporation's Ontario Book Initiative. We further
acknowledge the support of the Canada Council for the Arts and the Ontario Arts Council for
our publishing program.

Printed in Canada

1 2 3 4 5 6   10 09 08 07 06 05

For my brother, Matthew,

grandson of a foundling

Contents

Introduction

I grew up knowing that my father's parents were both orphans. They had been raised in different orphanages in London, England. That was all I knew. But I imagined many things for them: drab grey uniforms, grim dining halls with inedible food, thin pillows on cots in cavernous dormitories.

On the way to a family gathering in 2002, when my father was eighty-one years old, I finally thought to ask more about his parents.

"Dad," I said, "your father must have mentioned some little thing about the place where he grew up. About the food, or the other boys, or a favourite teacher. *Something!*"

"I don't think so," said my father. "Though he did refer to it as the George Handel Orphanage."

"As in George Handel the composer?"

"Yes."

That was all I needed – a key phrase for an Internet search. Back home, I typed in "George Handel Orphanage" and felt a prickle of anticipation. Could I possibly be unlocking the door to our lost family history?

Within minutes I discovered that, way back in 1749, George Frideric Handel had become interested in helping a London hospital that cared for homeless children. A man named Thomas Coram had established the hospital, and today there still existed an organization called the Coram Family. There was a website bearing the invitation "Contact Us".

I sent a message to the e-mail address. My father's father had been named Arthur Jocelyn, I wrote, and he'd probably been born in 1880. Was there any chance that records of his childhood might still exist?

I heard back within a few hours. The records were on file. Had I lived in London, I could have gone to the London Metropolitan Archives and looked them up for myself. But since I was writing from Canada, I would be put on

I do not remember my grandpa
Arthur Jocelyn at all. He died
nearly 50 years ago, when I was
two years old. My older cousins
remember calling him Papa
Jocelyn; Arthur was happy to
push the baby carriage holding
one of his grandchildren; he and
my grandmother often sang duets
for church and community events;
he planted a garden every spring
— that was really all I knew.

a waiting list until a staff member could find them for me. In the meantime, Arthur Jocelyn's immediate family — my aunt, then eighty-six years old, and my father — must send letters giving permission for the inquiry.

Many, many weeks went by.

Finally came a thick brown envelope postmarked London. It was addressed to my father and aunt, and the letter inside began:

> Your father was born on 27 September 1880 at 5 Royal Place, Greenwich, London. It was his mother's first confinement and she named your father John Graham Ranson.

Our surname wasn't really Jocelyn! But why had my grandfather's name been changed? Where had his poor mother come from? Who was his father? And why had my grandfather grown up in an orphanage if his parents were alive?

CHAPTER ONE

Castaway Children

 small crowd of women hovers outside the gates of a house in Hatton Garden, in the heart of London, England, on a Saturday evening in the spring of 1741. Most of the women have shawls shadowing their faces. All of them are carrying babies.

Mary Webb approaches along the road but hesitates when she sees how many people are here before her. She holds little Eliza closely, tugging on the skimpy flannel blanket, touching her nose against the downy hair on her infant daughter's head.

It was a dreadful decision to come here tonight. But Mary has nowhere else to go. She used to work as a housemaid, but her mistress called her terrible names when she found out that Mary was having a baby, and sent her away without even paying the wages still owed. Mary hasn't eaten in three days, except for a stale bun she found under a street cart.

She tiptoes toward the group of mothers and their babies. She glimpses other anguished faces, and knows that all the women are here because they are poor and alone. Many have probably been turned away by lovers and families. They too will have lost their jobs, they too have nothing to eat. Perhaps, for some of them, this gateway is the last desperate hope, before they give up and murder their own children. Only misery could have pushed them this far.

Mary and the other mothers have all come here tonight to leave their precious babies in the arms of strangers.

The mothers catch their breath when the gas light at the gateway is suddenly extinguished. They shuffle forward in the dark, clutching their babies tightly. Mary presses closer to the doorway, not looking at anyone else, keeping her gaze on Eliza's pale cheek and dark lashes.

One at a time, the women are admitted into the house.

Once inside, Mary is directed to a room on the right. A steward takes her baby, handing Mary the faded blanket, still warm from Eliza's body. Mary's eyes blur with tears as her child is carried away to be examined in another room. If Eliza is healthy enough, Mary will be dismissed without another chance to say goodbye.

She will probably never see her child again.

Perhaps Eliza will be recorded as Baby # 33: "a female child about two months almost naked a paper with it a pink ribboned knot."

Perhaps the woman behind Mary is whispering farewell to Baby # 46: "a male child about a fortnight old red and white cotton sleeves a linnen roller well-dressed."

Is it harder for a mother to give her baby away, or to keep her child, knowing that she has no pennies left to buy food?

As sorrowful as she is at saying goodbye, Mary trusts that Eliza has a better chance of being cared for here, among strangers, than if she stays with her own mother. That's why she is abandoning her child at this house in Hatton Garden — the Foundling Hospital.

The Foundling Problem

Abandoned babies – called foundlings – had been a problem for many years, especially in the cities – not just in England, but all over Europe. Rome, Venice, Amsterdam and Paris all had homes for foundlings, some dating back as far as the Middle Ages.

But in London, in the early 1700s, there was no safe refuge for abandoned babies. The Parish Council was obligated by law to accept destitute children. (A parish was the neighbourhood served by a church; each parish had a council that dealt with social problems.) But parish nurses were considered by many to be "killing-nurses." It was said that "no child ever came out of their hands alive." In those days nurses were not medically trained, and many were ignorant and irresponsible.

At this same period, though, a great many London women were having babies they could not or would not support. It was a time when more people were crowding into the big city than ever before, looking for work and hoping to find a better life than in the village or on the farm. Many of the young men became soldiers or apprentices, and many of the young women were servants in big houses owned by wealthy merchants or members of the nobility.

London in 1751, seen from the north. The dome of St. Paul's Cathedral, just this side of the Thames River, dominates the skyline. The Foundling Hospital (see arrow) is on the north edge of town.

These were the days before the Industrial Revolution. Machinery was very primitive. People travelled on land by foot or horse, as there were no cars or railroads; they crossed the sea by sailing ship, as steamships had not yet been invented. In many country areas, life went on as it had for centuries. In the fast-growing cities, though, crime and pollution grew worse every year. The streets were rank with garbage and human waste; drinking water was polluted; infectious diseases spread rapidly through overcrowded slums.

There were thousands of people with no job at all, however, perhaps living far from their homes and families, seeking out comfort and company wherever they could find them.

In those days, of course, there was no artificial birth control. Alcohol played a role in many unplanned pregnancies. Gin was such a popular drink that these years were nicknamed The Gin Craze. There were over six thousand places to buy gin in London, and some of the ads offered "drunkenness for a penny, dead drunkenness for tuppence" (two pence). So much drinking was bound to lead to trouble.

People who are "tipsy" don't always think carefully about their actions. Of course, alcohol was not always at the root of the problem. Romance often led to unwanted pregnancies rather than marriage, and many young women were left alone to bear the responsibility of having a baby to look after.

In this detailed engraving, titled Gin Lane, *William Hogarth illustrated the evils that might come from drinking too much gin. Note the woman on the right, pouring gin down a baby's throat.*

In Britain, "pence" was the old plural of "penny." Until Britain changed its currency in 1970, there were 12 pence in a shilling and 20 shillings (240 pence) in a pound. Amounts were written as pounds/shillings/pence (£/s/d). A guinea was worth 21 shillings. It was considered more fashionable to price items in guineas.

There was also a high incidence of women being taken advantage of by their employers. Rape was not uncommon, nor was seduction by a figure in authority.

In London society back then, a child outside of marriage was almost always considered to be the woman's fault. Sometimes her friends and family turned against her and she had no one to help care for her child. She was called a "fallen woman" (meaning fallen from goodness or virtue), and she would have great difficulty keeping her job or finding a new one. Certainly finding another man, to share her life and the responsibility of a child, would be next to impossible.

The Birth of a Hospital

No one would guess, looking at Thomas Coram's youth, that he would grow up to save thousands of lives. Thomas was born in the seaport of Lyme Regis, on England's south coast, where his father, John Coram, likely worked in the Customs office. Thomas was only six or seven years old when his mother died, and he had at least two brothers who died as infants.

When Thomas was eleven, and soon after his father remarried, the lad signed on as a ship's cabin boy and sailed away – possibly toward Newfoundland, where there was much trade with England. He lived aboard ships until he was sixteen, and then came home for a time, to apprentice as a shipwright (shipbuilder).

Thomas eventually settled in America, where he ran a shipbuilding business in Massachusetts. He married a Boston woman named Eunice Waite, but they did not have any children. Although it seems he never actually captained a ship, he was known respectfully as Captain Coram. For several years his hard work led to success. However, his strong opinions and Anglican religious beliefs made him unpopular. He finally returned to England for good when he was fifty-four years old, owing money and very disappointed at the outcome of his ten-year American venture.

But Thomas Coram did not waste time feeling sorry for himself. He was a clever man, though not well educated. War was raging in Europe, and his life had taught him to find practical solutions to problems. Knowing about the shipbuilding business on both sides of the Atlantic Ocean, he now made himself a reputation "for encouraging the importation of Naval Stores from her Majesty's Plantations in America." This meant that he saved money for the British Navy by suggesting that tar from American pine trees should be used to seal ship seams, instead of expensive Swedish tar. Other naval supplies such as hemp and masts were also cheaper in North America. Coram was able to earn some money, and make a few friends in English society as well.

When Thomas Coram retired from the ship business, he and Eunice moved to the London suburb of Rotherhithe, near the River Thames. This was before the days of organized garbage collection, and his daily walks took him past the dung heaps used by Londoners as garbage piles. He was horrified to see that, alongside carcasses of dogs and horses, unwanted babies were frequently abandoned and left to die. He resolved that he would somehow manage to provide a shelter where these children could be cared for, instead of being cast aside.

He began by trying to get support from some of the leading gentlemen in London society. He believed that the king would "grant a charter" – give royal permission to start a charity – if Coram could prove that an impressive group of supporters had pledged to donate money to this worthy cause. As he said in an urgent letter to the wealthy Duke of Bedford, "With what barbarity tender infants have been exposed and destroyed, for want of proper means of preventing the disgrace, and succouring the necessities of their parents. . . ." He did not expect his idea to receive as much opposition as it did. Some men thought that if they helped women who had become pregnant by accident, they would be encouraging other women to do the same. Others felt that there were more virtuous causes to support.

At last it occurred to Thomas Coram to appeal to the wives of these men, who would perhaps be more tender-hearted toward babies than their husbands. He addressed his appeals to these ladies, saying that he intended "to prevent the frequent murders of poor miserable infants at their birth" and "to suppress the inhuman custom of exposing newborn infants to perish in the streets." He pointed out that, as well as saving vulnerable children, his

William Hogarth's portrait of Thomas Coram is considered one of his best paintings. Hogarth honestly portrays the captain as a man so short that his feet dangle above the floor, wearing no wig – despite the fashion of the time – and holding the prized royal charter for the Foundling Hospital.

plan would nourish and train useful citizens. He expected to provide England with soldiers and sailors and servants at a time when war with France was looming.

His idea worked. Although it took seventeen years altogether, he finally gathered enough signatures on three petitions of support: one signed by ladies, one by gentlemen and the third by "Persons of Distinction," who included several dukes and earls. In the past, people had often been individually generous to worthy causes; Captain Coram was the first to realize that a group of interested people could achieve more by working together.

King George II signed a charter establishing "an Hospital for the Maintenance and Education of Exposed and Deserted Young Children" (The word "hospital" had a different meaning back then. It usually meant a home for long-term care of a specific population – soldiers, unwed mothers, orphans, the blind or the insane.) The Great Seal – scarlet sealing wax embossed with the king's own insignia – was affixed to the charter on October 17. This date, known as Charter Day, would become a holiday for the foundlings, celebrated every year in the same way as Christmas – with roast beef and plum pudding.

Part of the opening sentence from the royal charter reads:

Whereas, Our trusty and wellbeloved subject, Thomas Coram, gentleman, in behalf of great numbers of helpless Infants daily exposed to destruction, has by his petition, humbly represented unto Us, That many persons of quality and distinction, as well as others of both sexes (being sensible of the frequent Murders committed on poor miserable Infants, by their Parents, to hide their Shame, and the inhuman Custom of exposing new born Children to perish in the Streets, or training them up in Idleness, Beggary and Theft), have by Instruments in writing, declared their Intentions to Contribute Liberally towards the Erecting an Hospital, after the example of other Christian Countries, and for supporting the same, for the Reception, Maintenance and proper Education of such helpless Infants. . . .

Thomas Coram – who was by now in his seventies – could not operate the Foundling Hospital alone. He selected 375 men, including himself, to be governors of the hospital. The king approved the list, with no changes. Some governors were noblemen, such as the Duke of Bedford, who served as the first president; some were very wealthy, and others were prominent merchants or professionals such as doctors, attorneys and architects. There were no women, though it was admitted in the bylaws that

> we may receive the Assistance of the Fair Sex, who, although excluded by Custom from the Management of the publick Business, are by their natural Tenderness and Compassion peculiarly enabled to advise in the Care and Management of Children; and they may, without Trouble to themselves . . . communicate to any Governor . . . by a Memorandum put into the Charity Box, or in such Manner as they shall think fit.

The entire group of governors met only once a year after the hospital was up and running, but fifty of them were chosen to form the General Committee. This committee was involved in every detail of running the institution, from hiring staff to composing regulations to deciding on the children's diet and wardrobe. A subcommittee of four or five dedicated men spent every Saturday morning paying the bills and attending to immediate concerns.

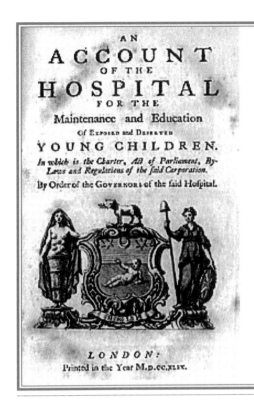

The governors wrote this 96-page "Account" in 1759. It includes a history and an outline of the Hospital's intentions, and regulations for raising infants "who are liable to be exposed to perish in the Streets, or be murdered by their indigent and inhuman Parents. . . ." William Hogarth designed the coat of arms, showing a naked baby under a shield held by the goddess Diana of Ephesus (with many breasts), symbolizing charity, and Britannia, symbolizing liberty. The crest is a lamb. The motto is simply "Help."

In the days before the Hospital opened in its first location – the house in Hatton Garden, in London – the governors and other well-wishers presented the institution with several gifts: medicine, the promise of free baptisms, a painted shield, a church Bible. Thomas Coram gave a large Common Prayer Book, the official book used in Anglican services.

Finally, opening night arrived. The Duke of Richmond was there, as well as the Hospital architect, Theodore Jacobsen, the painter William Hogarth and several other governors, including Captain Coram himself. The events were duly recorded, with the erratic punctuation and spelling that were common at the time:

> . . . At Eight o'Clock the Lights in the Entry were Extinguished, the outward Door was opened by the Porter, who was forced to attend at that Door all night to keep out the Crowd imediately the Bell rung and a Woman brought in a Child the Messenger let her into the Room on the Right hand, and carried the Child into the Stewards Room where the proper Officers together with Dr. Nesbitt and some other Govrs were constantly attending to inspect the Child according to the

Directions of the Plan. The child being inspected was received Number'd, and the Billet of its Discription enter'd by three different Persons for greater Certainty. The Woman who brought the Child was then dismissed without being seen by any of the Govrs or asked any Questions whatsoever. Imeadiately another Child was brought and so continually till 30 Children were admitted 18 of whom were Boys and 12 Girls being the Number the House is capable of containing. Two children were refused. One being too old and the other appearing to have the Itch.

. . . On this Occasion the Expressions of Grief of the Women whose children could not be admitted were Scarcely more observable than those of some of the Women who parted with their Children so that a more moving Scene can't well be imagined.

All the children who were received (Except Three) were dressed very clean from whence and other Circumstances they appeared not to have been under the care of the Parish officers, nevertheless many of them appeared as if stupifyed with some Opiate [drug], and some of them almost Starved, One as in the Agonies of Death thro' want of Food, too weak to Suck, or to receive Nourishment, and notwithstanding the greatest care appeared as dying when the Govrs left the Hospital which was not till they had given proper Orders and seen all necessary Care taken of the children.

Thomas Coram had been actively involved in the preparations for the Foundling Hospital, and after it opened he remained on the committee. But only a couple of years later, the other governors had a serious disagreement with him. Perhaps Coram's humble beginnings were what actually led them to accuse him of speaking indiscreetly about private Hospital business. It is hard to know now whether the accusation was fair, but there was enough hard feeling between Coram and the governors that they no longer respected his contributions. He was not re-elected to the governing committee. A friend of his, Dr. Brocklesby, wrote, "Free from all hypocrisy, he spoke what he thought with vehemence."

Coram's wife, Eunice, had died the year before the Hospital opened. Now at the end of his life, and with no children of his own, he was a lonely man who had spent all his savings on good works, and had been cast out of the community he had led for so long. He had helped so many people during his life that it seems especially sad that few people were now willing to help him.

This 1749 picture claims to show "an exact Representation of the Form and Manner in which EXPOSED and DESERTED Young children are Admitted into the FOUNDLING HOSPITAL." To avoid crowding and chaos at the gate, a lottery system had been introduced by this time. The woman on the right is holding a white ball and being welcomed. The woman near the left has a black ball and is being turned away. The woman in the centre is just drawing a ball from the sack. The fashionable people are watching these heart-wrenching events as a form of entertainment.

A few weeks after the death of his wife, Coram wrote this poignant letter to a friend.

It having pleased the Almighty God to remove my dearly beloved Wife from hence by death in the Middle of July Worn out by long Sickness, I was Marryed to her a little above 40 years during which time she never once gave me Cause to be angry or vexed at her, she was always a Sincere Christian of an humble meek and Quiet Spirit and Wisely Study'd my Peace and Comfort and was to her Life's End a virtuous kind and Prudent Wife without fault. She Chearfully bore an affectionate part in all my Toyls and affections. By her Death I am bereaved of one of the best of Wives.

He found solace by increasing his efforts on behalf of the needy, including planning another foundling hospital in Westminster. He continued to visit the children at the Hospital, however, and "he was often seen, clad in his well-worn red coat, seated on a bench under the Arcade, with tears in his eyes, regaling small Foundlings with gingerbread."

The end of Thomas Coram's story was inscribed in a stone epitaph in the southern arcade of the Hospital chapel:

> He died the 29th March, 1751, in the 84th year of his age;
> Poor in worldly estate, rich in good works,
> and was buried, at his own desire, in the Vault underneath this Chapel
> (the first there deposited) at the east end thereof,
> many of the governors and other gentlemen
> attending the funeral to do honour to his memory.

Thomas Coram's funeral was small but it was attended by the governors and a number of ladies and other gentlemen, all dressed in mourning clothes. A choir of children accompanied his body, in its plain elm coffin, from the courtyard to the burial vault.

Dr. Brocklesby wrote and circulated a lengthy pamphlet in memoriam that included this paragraph:

> The late Captain Thomas Coram . . . was a person whose merit and virtues were so extraordinary, exerted with such vigour, and with so great constancy to the benefit of society, that an attempt to raise some little monument to his memory, cannot fail of being well received by the public, whose servant he was for upwards of forty years before his death. . . .

Thomas Coram's Other Visions

The Foundling Hospital was not Thomas Coram's only humanitarian endeavour. The Reverend Samuel Smith, the man who had baptized many of the first foundling babies, wrote to a mutual friend of his admiration of Coram:

Later the Hospital moved to a permanent location. Thomas Coram's figure watched over the entrance for many years, until its head fell off! The statue was repaired but is now gone. The gates are still there, including the central alcove, where the porter often discovered a basket holding a baby.

Mr. Coram is animated with so generous and extensive a Zeal, that he has a share in forwarding the Progress of almost every good Undertaking, that is set on Foot by publick spirited Persons amongst us.

Even after his return to England, Coram's concerns in North America had continued. He had assisted a tribe of Mohicans in their struggle to reclaim land taken from them by the king. He had put great effort into a plan to educate girls in the New World. He believed that, if young native mothers were taught to read and write and to understand Christianity, they would be more likely to teach their children, thereby influencing the next generation of both sexes.

Coram also had a dream of establishing a colony in Nova Scotia, populated by artisans and demobilized soldiers and marines. His letter to King George II on this subject suggests

That the Coasts of your Majestie's Province of Nova Scotia afford the best Codd-fishing of any in the known parts of The World and the Land is well adapted for Raising Hemp & other Naval things For the better Supplying this Kingdom with the Same, But the Discouragements Have hitherto been such as have deterr'd People from

Settling there Whereby the said Province through want of good Inhabitants is not so beneficial to this Kingdom nor so well secured to the Crown as it might be. . . .

Although Coram's interest in the Nova Scotia colony diminished as he became more involved in the Foundling Hospital, he had the satisfaction of knowing that

in May, 1749, a fleet of eighty-four transports loaded with three thousand colonists . . . set sail for Nova Scotia. This time, the settlement project had been fathered by Lord Halifax, whose plan for the colony displayed many similarities to Coram's earlier schemes. The government had acted with extraordinary speed, and the result was the establishment of the town of Halifax in Nova Scotia.

On April 13, 1751 – ten days after Thomas Coram's funeral – *Read's Weekly Journal*, the *Penny London Post* and the *London Advertiser* all agreed that, at the time of his death, Coram had been pursuing a project that would employ "vagrants, idle persons and the distressed poor" – that is, people who were homeless, unemployed or otherwise needy – and that a building was shortly to be erected for this purpose. Right to the end, Thomas Coram – that motherless boy who had gone to sea when he was just eleven – was doing his best to help others.

CHAPTER TWO

Babies and Bookkeeping

hen the Foundling Hospital first opened its doors, in the house in Hatton Garden, it had room for thirty children. But some nights there were a hundred babies waiting for only a few places. Mothers like Mary Webb were frantic to be the first through the gate. This "gave rise to the disgraceful scene of women scrambling and fighting to get to the door."

The governors began to look for a larger, permanent site, amid fields and fresh air, farther from the roar of the city. They bought a piece of land north of London, in an area known as Lamb's Conduit Fields. (A man called Lamb had once built a water conduit there, hence the odd name.) The plan for the hospital included separate living quarters for girls and boys, separate dining halls, a large courtyard flanked by columned walkways, and a spacious Anglican chapel.

They also came up with a plan to control the crowd of parents fighting to gain admission for their children. On nights when spaces were available, they would advertise that fact. Then they would hold a sort of lottery. Each mother would be brought into the house and instructed to sit on a bench without moving. One by one, the mothers would be told to pull a coloured ball out of a sack.

All a mother's hopes depended on the colour of ball she happened to draw. A white ball meant that her child would be examined at once. A red ball put her child on the waiting list, in case a white-ball baby failed inspection. A black ball sent mother and child back into the streets.

The governors clearly knew how desperate the rejected mothers would be; they made arrangements with the local police to patrol the neighbourhood, to prevent these despondent women from simply abandoning their babies. The lottery system continued for fifteen years, with an average of ninety-two infants being admitted each year.

The new Foundling Hospital in Lamb's Conduit Fields was soon commonly referred to as "the Foundling." Construction was finished first on the west wing. The need was so great that the governors decided to open that section at once. There were 192 places, with each bed shared by two children. But another problem arose almost immediately. With the bigger facility there was space for more children, but there was not enough money to look after them all. Caring for so many children was expensive, even when their suppers were bread and butter and they each received only two new shirts a year.

After much effort, a solution was found. In 1756, while the Hospital was struggling to find supporters, Parliament agreed to endow the institution with the large sum of £10,000. However, certain conditions had to be met:

> The Foundling Hospital must accept every baby under two months old brought to its gates; this was described as General Reception.
>
> The hospital must be ready to receive babies at all hours, day and night.
>
> The inspectors must approve "60 Wet nurses and 20 Dry." (Wet nurses were nursing women who could breastfeed other women's babies.)
>
> A basket must be hung at the gate of the main entrance, "into which the mother, after giving the Porter notice by ringing the bell, could deposit her child."

One hundred and seventeen babies were placed in this basket by the entrance on the first night of General Reception. By the end of the first month, 425 babies had been left there!

Despite a flurry of preparations – such as the hiring of 140 wet nurses in the country, the purchase of twenty cradles, thirty beds and clothing for 500 infants – the Foundling Hospital was not quite ready for such a surge of admissions.

That a sum not exceeding 10,000£ be granted to H.M. to enable the Foundling Hospital to ~~admitt~~ receive all Children under a certain Age who shall be brought to them between the 24th of May & the 24. of Dec.r 1756.

This unofficial-looking note changed the history of the Foundling. By endowing the Hospital with £10,000, Parliament opened the doors to any and every child in need. The Hospital would take in nearly 15,000 babies in three years. Two-thirds of them would die.

General Reception caused many changes, most of them for the worse. It was now possible for anyone to drop off a baby. Sometimes, without the mother knowing, an unhappy father tried to leave a child he had no wish to support. The streets near the Foundling were frequently the setting for dramatic scenes, as parents argued bitterly over whether or not they should give up their baby.

Inside the gates, it was a struggle to keep order. Every baby had to be examined, baptized, clothed, numbered and sent to a nurse. And all these steps needed to be recorded accurately, in case someone made inquiries later about a particular child.

Babies, Babies, Babies

Infants admitted to the Hospital were immediately given new names. For this reason, the newspaper notice announcing that General Reception would begin on June 2, 1756, requested that those delivering babies should "affix on each child some particular writing, or other distinguishing mark or token, so that the children may be known thereafter if necessary." This was in case the parents were later capable of reclaiming their children and supporting them. The tokens – which remained in use until the end of the eighteenth century – were as varied as the children they represented.

Some were Latin phrases: *Vale, forte in aeternum vale, O chara* (Farewell, perhaps farewell forever, O beloved). Some were handmade: folded paper, knotted ribbons, small samples of embroidery. Some were metal tags etched with initials, or buttons, or coins, or rings or other jewellery. Many tokens were letters, some in verse, all expressing great sadness at the "cruel separation." Whatever form it took, each token was left in hopes of an eventual reunion, in better times, of the parent and the foundling.

Among the tokens listed in hospital records are:

#18127 A half Crown of the reign of Queen Anne, with hair
#18069 An old silk purse
#18070 A silver 4 pence and an ivory fish
#17110 A small gold locket

Children received new names when they entered the Foundling, but Hospital records linked them to any note or sketch or other token. The Handbook says, "Any writing or remarkable Thing, brought with Child, is to be sealed up immediately, and marked with the Letter of the Child on the Out-side." The children were never told that these mementos had been left behind. The Foundling Museum still has hundreds of them. Some sorrowful mother kept the other half of this drawing, hoping to reclaim her child someday. The sad little plea to the "worthey governors" is signed with an X beneath dictated words; the mother could not read or write.

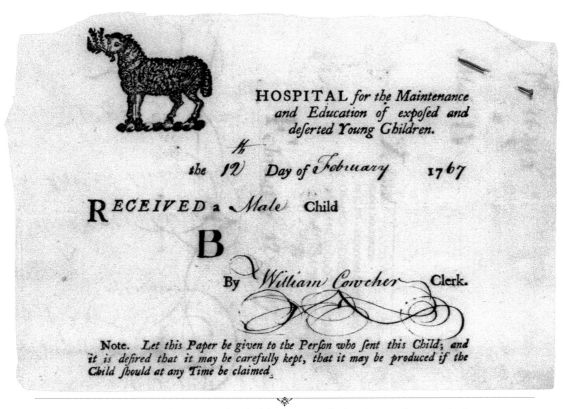

HOSPITAL *for the Maintenance and Education of expoſed and deſerted Young Children.*

the 12ᵗʰ Day of February 1767

RECEIVED a Male Child

B

By William Cowcher Clerk.

Note. *Let this Paper be given to the Perſon who ſent this Child; and it is deſired that it may be carefully kept, that it may be produced if the Child ſhould at any Time be claimed.*

This brusque receipt bearing a lamb (the Hospital's logo) served a practical purpose. If the mother was accused of having murdered her baby, she could prove she had in fact given it to the Hospital.

The first boy and girl to be baptized at the Foundling Hospital were named after Thomas and Eunice Coram. The next several babies were named after the governors, artists and various noblemen who supported the institution, like Albemarle, Bedford, Pembroke and Montague.

Next, the name choices moved on to "eminent deceased personages," "then came the mighty dead of the poetical race," such as Geoffrey Chaucer and William Shakespeare. A series of war heroes had foundling namesakes – for example, Oliver Cromwell and Francis Drake. Then painters were honoured: Peter Paul Rubens, Michelangelo, William Hogarth (along with his wife, Jane). During General Reception, when so many names were required that the governors ran out of famous people, "they took a zoological view of the subject, and named them after the creeping things and beasts of the earth."

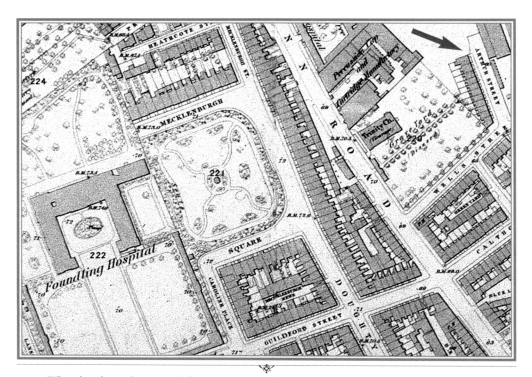

The chaplain christened the incoming babies. By the 1800s, new names were in such short supply that they were often selected from the London street directory. Perhaps Arthur Jocelyn was baptized this way. On this map, an Arthur Street can be seen in the upper right, not far from the Hospital; a Jocelyn Road (not in this picture) was a bit farther away. The entrance of the hospital was on Guildford Street; the walls enclosed a large lawn in front of the building complex.

The Perils of General Reception

By the end of five months of General Reception, over eight hundred babies had been taken in. The governors had been forced to hire more nurses, porters and other servants. Because there wasn't time for careful interviews, not all the new employees were suitable. On occasion, staff took bribes to sneak in babies who were over the limit of two months in age, or who had been brought from some district outside London.

Inspectors were hired to keep track of the foundlings in foster homes in villages outside London, but they too could sometimes be bribed to ignore bad living conditions, or more children in a family than were allowed.

The clothes worn by each arriving baby were carefully recorded on a list like this one. Birthmarks or scars were also noted.

No.

Child about _____ old

Marks and clothing:

Ribbons	Cloak	Mantle
Forehead Cloth	Upper-Coat	Pilch
Cap	Roller	Sleeves
Head-Cloth	Petticoat	Stockings
Bonnet	Bed	Blanket
Long-Stay	Bodice-Coat	Shoes
Biggin	Waistcoat	Neckcloth
Bibb	Robe	Marks On the
Gown	Shirt	Body
Handkerchief	Barrow	
Froc	Clout	

★ A baby today still wears a clout, but now it's called a diaper!

Even worse, unscrupulous people were making a profit at the expense of desperate mothers who paid to have their babies transported – usually by strangers – to London. According to the treasurer in 1759, "The children sent into the Hospital are many of them starved, and labouring under the worst distempers, and many of them actually dying at the time of Reception."

There were also alarming stories of children perishing on the journey. There was the tinker (pot-mender) who was paid a guinea to take a baby to the Foundling Hospital; the baby was later found drowned, with a stone fastened around its neck. Or the man hired to carry five infants in baskets from the country; he got drunk and fell asleep in a field, and by the time he woke up only two babies were still alive. Yet another story tells of a man transporting eight babies from several towns away. Only one baby survived that long ride, and that was because its mother walked behind the wagon for the entire journey, feeding her infant along the way.

During the period of General Reception, 14,934 children were received, and 10,204 died. Of those who died, 4,735 were under the age of six months;

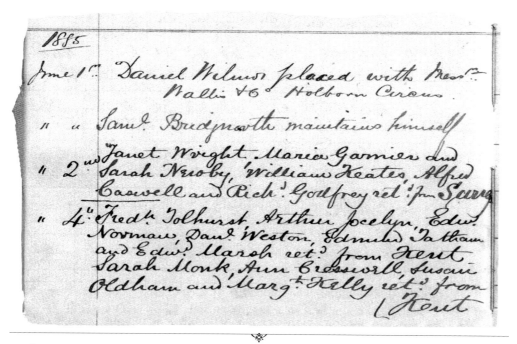

YEAR.	DAY OF RECEPTION.	HOSPITAL NUMBER.	SEX	NAME.	WHEN BORN.	REMARKS.
1881	5th July	21,841	M	Arthur Jocelyn	27th Sept 1880	Died
1881	26th July	21,842	F	Maria Garnier	27th Feby 1880 * see inside cover	Restored to her Mother Febry 26th 1896
1881	26th July	21,843	M	George Sparkes	27th Septr 1880 * see inside cover	
1881	27th September	21,844	M	Edward Norman	9th Jany 1881	

Arthur Jocelyn, born John Graham Ranson, was admitted to the Foundling Hospital on July 15, 1881, when he was nine months old. He was assigned the number 21,841. The girl listed below him, Maria Garnier, was admitted just three weeks later. She was apparently raised by the Foundling until the age of 16, when she was "Restored to her Mother." A few children were reclaimed by parents many years after their arrival, but it did not happen often.

1885

June 1st Daniel Wilmer placed with Messrs Wallis & Co Holborn Circus.

" " Saml Bridgnorth maintains himself

" 2nd Janet Wright, Maria Garnier and Sarah Newby, William Keates, Alfred Caswell and Richd Godfrey retd from Surrey

" 4th Fredk Tolhurst, Arthur Jocelyn, Edwd Norman, Danl Weston, Edmund Tatham and Edwd Marsh retd from Kent Sarah Monk, Ann Cresswell, Susan Oldham and Margt Kelly retd from Kent

On June 4, 1885, Arthur Jocelyn returns from his foster mother in Kent, along with several other children. The entry for June 2 mentions Maria Garnier returning from Surrey.

Although the Hospital saved money on staff by sending children to foster homes, there were still many costs involved. One important expense was the package given to each infant when it was sent to the country for fostering.

Each outfit consisted of: 4 Biggens, 4 long Stays, 4 caps, 4 neckcloths, 4 shirts and 12 clouts, and also the following woollen cloathing: a Grey Linsey mantle, a pair of Grey linsey sleeves, 2 white Bays Blanketts, 2 Rowlers, and 2 double Pilches.

A few months later, each child would be sent "a Grey Linsey Coat and Petticoat, and a Grey Linsey Boddice Coat."

971 between six months and one year; and 967 between the ages of one and two.

Despite all these horrors, it took over three years for everyone to realize that a new plan was needed to make the Foundling Hospital work as it should. Parliament finally admitted "that the indiscriminate admission of all children under a certain age into the Hospital had been attended with many evil consequences" and recommended "that it be discontinued."

The last child christened under this imperfect system was named, by the chaplain, Kitty Finis. In French, *finis* means "finished."

Foster Families

Although there were reports of unkind nurses and uncaring foster families, thousands of others did the job they were hired to do with the love and attention that every child needs. Some women fostered as many as twenty or twenty-five foundlings over the years.

Most foundlings were tiny babies when they were sent to live in the country with a wet nurse. They soon had no memory of their birth mothers, and grew up attached to the new families who took care of them.

What kind of household took in a stranger's baby and gave the child a home for four or five years?

In the early days the foster families were usually poor, and grateful to be paid a few extra shillings a week. The men worked on farms or in mines or at other labouring jobs. Many foster parents did not know how to read or write, though some taught their foundlings the alphabet. Often, their cottages were in small villages and had only one room, heated by a large fireplace. There would be a bed, a table and chairs, a storage chest, a few dishes and not much more. There could be several children in the home, some foundlings and some not. The family might be lucky enough to have an outdoor privy (outhouse), or their waste might be tossed into the street. There were usually other village children for the foundlings to play with, and plenty of fields to roam.

Most of the foundlings loved their foster mothers as their own, and the mothers were often very reluctant to let them go when the time came. For the children, leaving a cozy family and arriving at the huge Foundling Hospital, swarming with strangers, must have been a harsh shock.

One foundling, Charles Nalden, left a record of his last day in his foster home:

> My mother had the good sense to give me periodic reminders that one day I must leave home, to live in the big "orspiddle" in London. Thanks to her unfailing love and plain common sense, the wrench, when ultimately it did come, proved not nearly so great a shock as it would otherwise have done. Once my sixth birthday had passed, I knew that time was rapidly running out. The dreaded day came. . . . It started with my mother hanging around my neck the bone locket on which was stamped my Foundling Hospital number – 23062. . . .

During those years of foster care, the inspectors kept an eye on the children, and reported to the Hospital matron. According to General Committee minutes:

> in 1802 Mr. Vine reports to Mrs. Pope on the 68 children in his care: 48 were "Fine Children," 9 were "Thriving," 3 recovering from Measles, 7 "Weakly" and 1 dead.
>
> In 1813 Mr. Vine reports to Matron: 67 Fine healthy children, 7 weakly and indisposed, 2 convalescent, 2 supposed to be weak in intellect, 1 ideot, 1 subject to fits, 1 with crooked ancles, 1 with a speck in one of its eyes.

In 1815 Mr. Living reports to Matron: 66 Fine children, 8 in poor health, 5 weakly, 1 diseased finger, 1 deformed in back, 2 deformed in legs, 1 bad legs.

Hogarth and Handel

Over the years, many famous people took a special interest in the children of the Foundling Hospital. Two of them were the celebrated artist William Hogarth, and the great composer George Frideric Handel.

In 1707, when William Hogarth was ten years old, his father was arrested for not paying his bills. Richard Hogarth had been a teacher who dreamed of opening a coffeehouse where only ancient Greek and Latin were spoken. When he finally opened this classical café, the idea proved to be hopelessly unpopular, and he lost all his money and more. The family was deeply in debt.

In those days, this meant that the whole family was sent to live in the Fleet debtors' prison until Richard could pay back the money he owed. This horrible place was built beside the Fleet Ditch – a river so polluted from being used as a sewer and toilet that the dreadful stink never left the air.

When the family was released after more than four years, in 1712, and William had reluctantly finished school, the youth began working for a silver-plate engraver. His main task seems to have been engraving "shopcards" – small advertisements for merchants. He found the work repetitive and uninspiring, and may not have quite completed his seven-year apprenticeship.

By 1720, young William was finally ready to set up his own engraving shop. Eventually he produced satirical prints mocking the lively social world that surrounded him. He invented a new form of art, one that told a story in a series of six or eight drawings, attacking injustice, praising goodness or poking fun at wealthy show-offs.

Hogarth was also an excellent portrait painter, but because he insisted on painting people as they truly were, he could not always find customers!

He became friends with Thomas Coram, and his painting of Coram (see Chapter 1) displays his usual frank style. He also got involved in the development of the Foundling Hospital. Perhaps the upsets of his own childhood made him sympathetic to abandoned children.

During the construction of the building at Lamb's Conduit Fields, Hogarth had an idea that no one had thought of before. He "contemplated

The March of the Guards to Finchley, *by William Hogarth. The artist donated
this painting for a lottery to raise money for the Foundling Hospital. As it turned out,
the Hospital held the winning ticket! Hogarth's friend Mr. Justice Welsh described the
scene in detail: "Near the centre of the picture . . . is a handsome young grenadier
[soldier] in whose face is strongly depicted repentance mixed with pity and concern;
the occasion of which is disclosed by two females putting in their claim for his person.
. . . The figure upon his right hand . . . is a fine young girl . . . debauched with child,
and reduced to the miserable employ of selling ballads. . . ."*

*King George II – who still had his father's German accent – was very unhappy with
the satire of his army, and responded, "I hate bainting and boetry too! Neither the
one nor the other ever did any good! Does the fellow mean to laugh at my guards?"*

This painting, The Foundling Restored to Its Mother, *by Emma Brownlow King, shows an imaginary scene of a mother reclaiming her child. The Hospital secretary is the painter's father, John Brownlow (see Chapter 6). Note the mother's receipt for the child lying on the floor, along with toys she has brought for her daughter. The paintings on the wall – including Hogarth's* March to Finchley, *and portraits of Shakespeare and Ben Jonson – are still part of the Hospital's art collection. A few months after the picture was painted, this little girl really was reclaimed by her mother.*

the adornment of its walls with works of Art, with which view he solicited and obtained the cooperation of some of his professional brethren." In today's words, this meant that he realized how the Hospital – and the children – would benefit from works of art hanging on its large, bare walls. He donated some of his own work, and asked friends and colleagues to do the same. Almost by chance, William Hogarth's generous instinct created the first public exhibition space in Britain. A fellowship grew up among the artists, who looked for other opportunities to show their work together and contribute to society. They established an artists' group that still exists, and is known as the Royal Academy of Arts.

William Hogarth was one of the original governors of the Hospital. He designed the coat of arms, as well as the uniforms for the children. He became an inspector of the wet nurses who cared for infants in Surrey and Kent. Like the Corams, he and his wife, Jane, had no children of their own, but they became foster parents to a number of foundlings.

In or about the year 1760, the Governors at the request of Hogarth, sent several of these poor Infants to Chiswick, where the painter resided, he engaging, along with Mrs. Hogarth, to see them properly taken care of.

One puzzle is that when William Hogarth died, in 1764, Jane Hogarth sent two foundlings back to the Hospital, where a receipt for their return remains on record.

George Frideric Handel's contribution was more professional than personal, but also vital. Without him, it is possible that the Foundling Hospital would have lasted only twenty years instead of two hundred.

Handel was born in the German city of Halle, in 1685. Despite the objections of his father, a barber-surgeon, the boy was devoted to music, and he became the organist for the Halle cathedral when he was only seventeen. One of his professors was the founder of an orphanage, probably inspiring Handel's later dedication to the Foundling.

After a stay in Italy, where he began to compose operas, Handel moved to London when he was about twenty-five years old. There he developed a new style of performance called the oratorio. Before this, operas were entirely sung. They had elaborate sets and often dramatic choreography. In Handel's new events, there was no staged action. An oratorio contained choral music and operatic sequences as well as dialogue or narration.

Slowly, Handel established a fine reputation in England. He was hired by King George II to create *Music for the Royal Fireworks*.

By 1749, Handel was famous. He "Generously & Charitably offered a Performance of Vocal and Instrumental Musick" to help pay for the completion of the chapel at the Lamb's Conduit Hospital. The event was such a success that he returned the following spring. On May 1, 1750, he conducted an oratorio that had been heard in London only twice before, without much success. On this occasion the *Messiah* was received with huge excitement; over the years it became his most enduring masterpiece. Handel repeated the performance every year until 1759, when he conducted the *Messiah* for

George Frideric Handel was a staunch supporter of the Foundling Hospital. When his Messiah *was first performed at the Hospital, the Prince and Princess of Wales attended, and the concert proceeds were used to finish construction of the chapel. Performances of the* Messiah *were so popular and crowded that one invitation to the Hospital requested that gentlemen: "come without swords and the Ladies without Hoops." It was the only way to fit everyone in!*

the last time, one week before he died. These concerts raised thousands of pounds altogether, and probably saved the Hospital from closing.

Handel was elected as a governor of the Hospital and presented the institution with an organ for the chapel. He also composed several works especially for performances in the chapel. One of these was "The Foundling Hospital Anthem," which appears on several of the children's concert programs. It opens with these words:

Blessed are they who considereth the poor, the poor and needy,
    The Lord will deliver them in the time of trouble,
    The Lord preserve them and comfort them.

CHAPTER THREE

Growing Up at the Foundling

n the words of Hannah Brown, who wrote a book about her experiences as a foundling during the 1860s and 1870s, "Every child placed in the Foundling Hospital is twice deprived of a mother" – first its birth mother, and then its foster mother. The hardest day most children ever knew was the day when they said goodbye to the women who had become their mothers. Foundlings who have been interviewed all remember that arriving at their new home at the Hospital was sad and very frightening.

Children arriving back from the country were kept in the "Babies' Ward" for several days while their "Charity" uniforms were being made by the older students. Both boys and girls had their hair shorn off, probably to guard against lice, and they were instantly introduced to the somewhat military style of life in a large institution.

As well as losing their hair, their own clothing and their mothers, the foundlings also said goodbye to the outside world for the next ten years.

But there was rarely time for much sympathy; the matrons were too busy looking after so many children (and, according to some accounts, too mean). The children aged five, six and seven lived in what was called the Infant School, apart from the older ones. The boys were placed in wards to the left and the girls to the right. From the first day on, there was very little

The governors ruled the Hospital from their elegant "court room," where their meetings were held, as well as any functions that included outside visitors. The elaborately sculpted plaster ceiling, chandelier, marble fireplace and wooden mouldings add to the lush effect. The walls were hung with pieces from the Hospital's fine art collection. Many of the paintings featured children or stories from the Bible. By opening the picture collection to public view, the governors drew in more potential sponsors.

communication between boys and girls. Foster siblings – those who had lived as brother and sister at their foster homes – were rarely allowed to talk to each other. Even the babies and children who died were buried separately according to their sex.

Early in the morning, the children got up at the ringing of the house bell. They dressed, made their beds, rinsed their hands, brushed their hair and said their prayers. After breakfast they were taught to read and allowed outdoor playtime. The governors felt that healthy children with strong characters were most likely to emerge from a rigorous, supervised routine. In the Infant School, even visiting the bathroom was done on a schedule. One of the privileges of moving to the Upper School was using the toilet when you needed to.

The "infants" had special Sunday services in their own wing, and also learned the important task of darning (mending) socks. Charles Nalden, a Foundling resident from 1913 to 1921,

> soon discovered that there could be few discomforts in life greater than that caused by badly darned socks; for twist and turn one's toes and feet as one will, there is no escaping the hard little knots resulting from badly darned socks.

Because all the socks went into the laundry together, there was no guarantee of ever wearing the same socks again. They all learned to darn as best they could!

The children's daily routine in the Upper School at the beginning of the 1800s was described by Sir Thomas Bernard, treasurer at that time:

> They rise at six in the summer and daylight in winter, part of them being employed before breakfast in dressing the younger children, in cleaning about the house, and the boys in working a forcing pump which supplies all the wards and every part of the Hospital abundantly with water. At half past seven they breakfast and at half after eight into school, where they continue, the boys till twelve, the girls a little later. At one o'clock they dine, and return to school at two, and stay till four in the summer and in winter till dusk, except on Saturday when they have half-holiday. They are also instructed in singing the Foundling Hymns and anthems, and in their catechism, and are occasionally employed in and about the house during play-hours. At six in the evening they sup and at eight go to bed . . . the boys and girls are kept entirely separated. The girls are divided into three classes, under the care of three different mistresses, in needlework and reading. The elder girls are also employed in household work, and assist as servants in the kitchen, laundry and other rooms in the canteen wing.

> The little boys knit the stockings that are wanted for the children in the house: the elder boys, in their turn, work in the garden and assist as servants in their own wing and in working the pump and cleaning the court yard at the Chapel. They are all taught, and make a proficiency in, reading, writing and accounts. Different occupations and manufactures have been, at times, introduced into the Hospital. The last that has been

tried, with much effect and continuance, has been the spinning of worsted yarn. It was, however, attended with this inconvenience, that the boys who had been so employed were not so much in request as apprentices and were not placed out so speedily, or as well, as those whose writing, reading and accounts had been more attended to, and who have occasionally been employed about the house and garden.

Each dormitory slept about fifty children, two in each bed for the first hundred years. The sharing stopped in 1840, when the Board of Health recommended that sleeping alone could be a precaution against the spread of disease and infestation: "That all the wooden bedsteads be disposed of and replaced by iron bedsteads, and that every child have a separate bed."

Keeping clean was done in military style. According to a foundling named Harvey,

> There were bowls with stone slabs around and this was the routine. One of the bigger boys had the soap and a scrubber and it was: palms down, scrub, scrub – palms up, scrub, scrub – thumbs together, scrub, scrub. Like that.

At night, the nurse and an older foundling efficiently washed the necks of all the little ones lined up at the sink. On bath night, dozens of children were washed in the same water, which grew cold and scummy by the end of the evening. Several bodies were plunked into the bath together and their heads pushed under by force. The bigger ones would scoop the children out, dry them off and hurry them into their nightdresses. "After this operation," noted Hannah Brown, "each child got into bed and covered itself up, having no mother to kiss and say 'Good Night' to."

Five years after the Foundling's opening, there is a note in the minutes responding to a fad of sightseers visiting the dormitories to watch the foundlings sleep:

> That the Committee having been Informed That several Persons came to see the Children after they were in Bed, which disturbing their Rest, Resolved That the Bell be rung for the Children in this Hospital to go to Bed at Seven in the Evening and the Wards to be cleared and locked up at half an hour after Seven, and no person is to be admitted into the said Wards after that Hour.

The hundreds of children accepted during the years of General Reception began to return from fostering in the mid-1760s. The Foundling quarters could not possibly house them all, and Parliament's funds were used, in part, to open a series of "branch" hospitals "in counties remote from London," in districts with abundant opportunities for apprenticeships in the garment industry or in farming. In general, the costs were lower than in the city, and the country air was considered healthier for the children. However, when the flow of foundlings began to dwindle, the country branches were closed down, one by one.

In theory the children were allowed to write to their foster families. In practice, according to Hannah Brown, such letters never varied in composition, because they needed approval before they could be posted. The approved text was:

Dear Mother,
I now have the greatest pleasure in writing these few lines to you, hoping to find you quite well and happy, as it leaves me at present.
Please give my love to all the Family.
I remain,
Your affectionate girl. . . .

From Head to Toe

After the first foundlings were sent off to their nurses with little bundles of baby clothes, the governors didn't think again about dressing them until they came back four or five years later. William Hogarth's design for the Hospital uniform in about 1745 set the tone for two hundred years. Although the girls' snugly stiffened bodices loosened and skirt lengths changed over time, foundling fashion was generally way out of date. This didn't matter too much, because the children's exposure to the outside world was limited and they were not aware of looking peculiar – until they left the institution.

This sketch of a foundling boy and girl, dating from 1747, shows Hogarth's design for their uniforms. The later portraits, done in 1914, show how little the outfits changed. After 200 years the girls' skirts and the boys' jackets were shorter, but they remained brown with red trim and brass buttons until the very end.

From the beginning the colour scheme of the children's clothes was brown trimmed with red, and from the beginning the Governors ordered them made of good, sturdy woollen cloth; coats of brown drugget for all of the children, dresses of brown serge for the girls. For shifts and shirts the Hospital used Lancashire sheeting, and for the girls' caps, Irish linen. And the children had to wear shoes and stockings. In 1757 the Governors decided that both boys and girls should wear low-heeled shoes, and in 1760 the matron devised a new style of bodice for the girls, one made without any stiffening except buckram. But apart from this, the uniform apparently underwent very few changes in the course of the century.

Their uniforms were kept in baskets at the end of each bed. The outfits could not have been very comfortable. The drugget used in the coats, for example, is defined in Webster's dictionary as "a coarse durable cloth usually of wool mixed with linen, jute or cotton used chiefly as a lining or protective covering for carpets . . . made from fleece of wire-haired sheep of India."

Along with unscheduled bathroom visits and being allowed to use knives at meals, another benefit of entering the Upper School, according to Charles Nalden, was

going into long trousers. . . . Our new uniform comprised a "bum-freezer" jacket and pocketless trousers (made from a thick, dark-brown woollen material), red waistcoat, white starched collar, black bow tie and "blucher" boots [named after a Prussian soldier, Field Marshal Blücher]. Our jackets and waistcoats boasted six brass buttons apiece, each of them bearing an embossed figure of a lamb. . . . All six waistcoat buttons had to be fastened, but a quaint custom ordered that the jacket's top button only be done up.

As for the girls,

their lace-up boots were certainly more elegant and stylish than the boys' ugly steel-studded bluchers. On Sundays the girls' off-white cali-co aprons would be exchanged for spotlessly white "Tippets and Aprons" (an innovation of the year 1793), and the elbow-length sleeves of their dresses trimmed with white bands of the same material. All this was set off by a quaintly designed white bonnet, exclusive to girls of

The Christening, *another painting by Emma Brownlow King, is set in front of the altar, though it is unlikely that baptisms really took place there. In the beginning, babies were admitted to the Hospital on Saturday night and those still alive on Sunday were baptized at the morning service. Later on, baptisms were moved to the evening to avoid prolonging the morning service. In 1809 the governors voted to end public baptisms and make the ritual a private one. Note the girls' white tippets (capes), aprons and sleeve-bands.*

the hospital. Their hair, which was worn in plaits [braids] during the week, fell loosely down their backs. The overall effect was charming.

Charles also notes that "An unsuccessful attempt was made in 1922 to replace our 18th century uniforms by a style of dress more in keeping with the times. . . ."

According to Ken Budden, a foundling from 1938 to 1948, even as late as 1948 the foundlings were dressed in a version of the same two-hundred-year-old uniform:

the collarless jacket and trousers were chocolate brown in colour, brass buttons to fasten the jacket, and underneath we wore a bright red waistcoat with brass buttons. On Sundays (and maybe special occasions) we donned a large stiff white collar for church. Of course we considered it the norm, being we were fairly isolated from the public.

The children received new clothes each year, before the governors' annual meeting in May. The governors took an interest in the tiniest details of the wardrobes, and there are several notes regarding them in their meeting minutes over the years:

1749: "the Boy's Hatts have for the future a Red Twist only without any knot round them instead of the Ferrit which they now wear."

1753: a list indicates that the governors provided enough changes to ensure cleanliness: every year each girl received three bib-aprons, three shifts, two night and two day caps, and each boy received three shirts. When a boy left to begin an apprenticeship, the governors gave him a coat, waistcoat, breeches, three shirts, two pairs of stockings, two pairs of shoes and a hat. The girls received a coat, two petticoats, three shifts, three day caps, two night caps, two bibs and aprons, two pairs of stockings, two pairs of shoes and a hat.

1774: Mercy Draper, a girl with a lovely voice, was sent out of the Hospital to sing in an oratorio for Mr. Stanley, a composer and the organist at St. Andrew Holborn Church. She would be staying overnight as a guest in his home. The governors decided to provide her with a special performance costume, but insisted that she travel in her uniform because "if the concert Dress were seen at the Hospital, it may have a bad effect on the other Children."

1776: it was ordered that the girls be taught to make and mend their own clothes, shoes excepted. Boys should be taught to mend their own clothes, linens and shoes excepted. The girls mended all their own bed linens, which were numbered to keep track. (By this time, the employees and older girls made most of the clothes – which brought down the cost of dressing so many children, though the materials still needed to be either manufactured or purchased.)

1790: the governors directed that "the children change their body linen [slips and undershirts] twice a week."

1793: the girls were given white aprons to wear on Sundays.

One of Hannah Brown's strongest memories was that, during her time at the Foundling Hospital, the girls were not provided with underwear:

> . . . though our clothes were all made of thick woollen material, not one fitted close to the body. They were gathered full round the waist, and were minus a certain undergarment.

She helped out with the five-year-olds coming in from their foster families, and described an encounter with a new small arrival:

> I was very much impressed with the clothes she was wearing, especially with a dainty pair of white knickers (these would be taken away within a day or so, to be minus that garment for the rest of her time in the Institution).

Hannah makes a third reference to this lack when she describes arriving at her first job, as a maid in a big house. Her new mistress oversaw her unpacking, as instructed by the Foundling Hospital, and was astonished by the disgraceful absence of underwear. With so much time and concern spent on the children's wardrobes, how could something so fundamental be omitted?

Feeding Hungry Mouths

Like everything else at the Hospital, the foundling diet was strictly regulated. The menu changed very little during two hundred years. The children ate plain food, with an emphasis on bread – except in 1800, during a war against Napoleon, when the committee "Resolved Unanimously":

> That it is the Duty of the Members of this Corporation, in Obedience to his Majesty's Proclamation, to adopt immediately every practicable measure for diminishing the consumption of Bread within the Walls of this Hospital.

Accounting of Shoes

1782

		L	s	d
March 24	489 pair of shoes remaining	63.	1.	4
	Paid for 3485 Pair of Shoes from the 24 March 1782 to 29 June 1784 being 120 weeks	460.	8	
		523.	9.	4

1784

		L	s	d
June 29	There remained 112 Pair of New Shoes The cost of which is to be deducted	16.	10	
		506.	19.	4
	3862 Pair of Shoes worn out from 24th March 1782 to 29th June 1784 Sold at 1/6 per doz. to be deducted	24.	2.	9
	Expense of Shoes	482.	16.	7
	Average # of children from 24th March 1782 to 29th June 1784 was 297			

In 1802 this ruling was changed: "as the price of bread has fallen the children have Bread and Cheese for supper 6 days a week and on Thursday they have the Rice porridge continued with the omission of Raisins and Currents."

Boys and girls were, of course, kept apart during meals. During the 1700s, the girls'
dining hall was lined with the largest of the donated portraits by contemporary artists.
These were later replaced by varnished panels inscribed with the names of benefactors
— a decoration repeated in the boys' hall — listing names, dates and amounts of
gifts to the hospital. In both dining rooms, the view out of the windows
was much preferred to the view of the wall.

The records of the General Committee show us exactly what the
foundlings were eating in 1762, and in 1790. Gruel and milk
porridge or pottage were similar, nearly liquid foods: a cereal such as
oatmeal or barley, boiled in water or milk. Dinner was eaten at midday,
and the children had a light supper in the evening.

1762

	Breakfast	Dinner	Supper
Sunday	Bread & Butter	Roast Beef & Greens	Milk Porridge
Monday	Gruel	Potatoes or Parsnips mash'd with Milk	Bread & Milk
Tuesday	Milk Porridge	Boiled Beef & Greens	Broth
Wednesday	Bread & Milk	Stewed Shins of Beef & Broth with Herbs & Roots	Milk Porridge
Thursday	Gruel	Mutton & Greens	Broth
Friday	Milk Porridge	Stewed Shins of Beef & Broth with Herbs & Roots	Bread & Cheese
Saturday	Bread & Milk	Rice Pudding	Gruel

1790

	Breakfast	Dinner	Supper
Sunday	Bread & Butter	Roast Beef & Vegetables	Bread & Cheese
Monday	Milk Pottage	Boiled Mutton & Vegetables	Bread & Butter
Tuesday	Bread & Butter	Boys: Rice Pudding Girls: Mutton Broth thickened with rice	Bread & Butter
Wednesday	Milk Pottage	Boiled Beef & Vegetables	Bread & Butter
Thursday	Milk Pottage	Broth thickened with Peas	Bread & Cheese
Friday	Milk Pottage	Boiled Mutton & Vegetables	Bread & Butter
Saturday	Bread & Butter	Boys: Broth Girls: Rice Pudding	Bread & Cheese

...pence of Diet for the Children of The Foundling Hospital.

...eakfast, Milk Pottage every Day in the Week except Sunday viz.[t]

9 Gallons Milk at /7[d]	„ 5 . 3	
1/2 Peck Oatmeal at 1/6	„ „ 9	
10 halfpeck Loaves at /10	„ 8 . 4	
Breakfast P[r] Diem	„ 14 . 4	
Multiply by	6	
	£4 . 0 „	

Breakfast on Sunday, Bread & Butter, viz:

10 Half peck Loaves at /10	„ 8 . 4	
12 lb. Butter at /8[d]	„ 8 „	„ 16 . 4
Breakfast P[r] Week: - - - - -		5 2 4

...ner Monday

6 Gallons Milk at /7[d]	„ 3 „ 6	
4 lb. Barley at /1 3/4	„ „ 7	
8 Loaves at /10	„ 6 . 8	„ 10 . 9

Tuesday

1/2 lb. Meat for each of 360 Child: 180 lb at /3 1/2	2 . 12 . 6	
8 Loaves to D[o] at /10[d]	„ 6 . 8	2 . 19 . 2

Wednesday

18 lb. Suet at /3 1/2	„ 5 . 3	
3 1/2 Bushels Flour at 6/	1 . 1 „	
18 Gallons Milk at /7[d]	„ 10 . 6	
1/2 lb. Ginger at 1/	„ „ 6	1 . 17 . 3

---

*Despite the careful accounting of every penny paid out to care for the foundlings,
their diet was missing some essential nutrients. The lack of vitamins A, C and D
probably contributed to frequent cases of weak eyesight, scurvy-like illnesses
and leg deformities. An official report declared that "few, if any, of the children
brought up in this hospital attain an average height."*

Hannah Brown refers to the menu changing slightly with the arrival of a
new matron: the children began to receive sausages once a week, and "occasionally we had jam! This we had never tasted before, and I remember it was
raspberry jam." She adds, "We were always hungry!"

Some of the older children went on brave food-finding missions. They
slipped the bread from Sunday dinner into their pockets and then sneaked into
the kitchen to dip the chunks in dripping from the roasts. They scraped out
the pots used to cook rice. They raided the garden and stole pea-shells, green
gooseberries, raw rhubarb and turnips, trying to fill their empty stomachs.

It's interesting to compare the children's regular diet to the other end of the scale. Here's the menu for an anniversary dinner the governors enjoyed in 1765.

First Course

Turbot with Lobster Sauce
Westmoreland Hams from 16–18 pounds each
Dishes of Chicken, 2 Roast and 2 Boiled
Pigeon Pies
Dishes of Calves head, hashed

Second Course

Dishes of Sweet Bread & Pigeons
Dishes of Asparagus, one hundred in a dish

Dessert

Tarts, Jellies, Cream, Blanc-Mange

More than a century after Napoleon, when Britain was at war against Hitler, Ken Budden noted that not much had changed: "My comments about the food are very short: Insufficient, unappetizing and ghastly. I suppose one must make allowances for the war being on."

Though their food may have been monotonous and scanty, the foundlings probably still ate far more meat, and had a better-balanced diet, than poor children outside the Hospital, who would be lucky to have roast beef once a year. In the early years, the foundlings also ate potatoes far more often than the general population. A vegetable garden on the Hospital grounds added greens to the diet from time to time. Chicken, fresh fruit and dessert were rarely served.

Sunday Dinner

Just as the baby selection lottery was an entertainment for the nobility in the early days, Sunday dinner at the Foundling became a popular attraction that

This painting – A Foundling Girl at Christmas Dinner, by Emma Brownlow King – shows a child enjoying an unusually generous meal. The children were permitted a half-pint of weak beer on Sundays and on feast days, and on Christmas they also had plum puddings and potatoes without their skins – a rare pleasure. For Christmas the dining hall was decorated, and there were sometimes oranges or pennies and party crackers as extra treats.

continued until 1926, when the Hospital moved out of London and into the countryside.

Sunday morning services in the chapel were open to the public, and usually attracted a large crowd. The governors originally resisted the temptation to rent pews to wealthy parishioners, but eventually recognized that this could be a good source of income. The foundlings sang, beautifully, music by Handel, Mozart, Haydn and Purcell. Afterwards, everyone herded into the dining halls to watch the children eat the only two-course meal they received each week.

This zoo-like practice was not discouraged by the staff. Perhaps one of the wealthy onlookers would be moved enough to donate a useful sum of money, or to sponsor a couple of foundlings as apprentices. Against the rules, nurses sometimes urged the foundlings to request money from the visitors.

But the children themselves seem to have despised being put on display. According to Hannah Brown,

In those days the Chapel was crowded with a fashionable congregation, who, after the service thronged into the dining hall, to see the children

Sunday at the Foundling Hospital, *done by H. Townley Green in 1872,*
shows fashionable ladies of London touring the girls' dining hall, amusing themselves
by picking out "aristocratic faces." The children were forbidden to speak while at
the table. Usually, the only "distinguishable noise during meal-times was
that created by the munching of 200 sets of young jaws."

eat! . . . The teacher in charge had a small mallet in her hand: as soon as
we had filed into the room, she rapped on the table to which we all
turned: rap! We put up our hands and closed our eyes: rap! A girl in the
centre of the room said Grace; one more rap, and we climbed into our
seats. We grew to hate our Sunday dinner-time, and as some of us grew
older, we left our dinner untouched on Sundays.

Charles Nalden described a similar scene taking place fifty years later:

For the sensitive foundling girl and boy this Sunday dinner meal could be a distressing and embarrassing experience; for as I have said, Sunday was visitors' day.

Grace having been sung to the accompaniment of the brass quartet on their professionally-polished instruments, a tap by the gavel denoted that we sit down. The moment we sat, boys would commence piling salt, not on to their plates (which had yet to be brought round) but on to their hunks of bread. It was a practice which embarrassed me greatly. Visitors would wander freely around our tables, pointing out a squint-eyed boy here, or maybe twins there. Should I sense that I was being singled out for discussion, I would blush most furiously.

He also says, "The only meal of the year which boasted eggs on the menu was Good Friday dinner, when we were served with one hard-boiled egg apiece."

Hannah Brown also remembers the opportunities sometimes presented:

Some of the visitors would take notice of certain children – usually the pretty ones – and bring them sweets: unless these were eaten up before leaving the table, they would be taken away from them after dinner by the Monitors: These were two bigger girls from Upper School who would usually make a systematic search of the Infants after dinner. A little piece of binding worn round the sleeve of the children's dress was a good receptacle for a stray sweet sometimes – as they were very hard to part with.

One of the blessings said before dinner at the Foundling was

Father of mercies, by whose love abounding
All we thy creatures are sustained and fed,
May we while here on earth thy praises sounding,
Up to thy heavenly courts with joy be led.

Here are the ingredients of those plum puddings
the children were served at Christmas:

100 lbs. plums

40 lbs. suet

20 gallons milk

25 lbs. sugar

2 lbs. allspice

2 lbs. ginger

4 bushels flour

Before you try making this at home, note that it makes
488 pounds (222 kilos) of pudding!

Learning Lessons

lthough saving the lives of abandoned children was the main purpose of the Foundling Hospital, Captain Coram had had another intention when he began his project: to educate future citizens so that they could contribute to society and add to the greatness of England.

The first step in this plan was to teach the foundlings how to read and do simple arithmetic. In the early days, the governors declared that teaching them to write as well was not a good idea; a resolution passed in 1754 firmly insisted that "None of the children of this Hospital be instructed in writing." Knowing how to write might allow these youngsters to forget their low beginnings in life, might encourage them to become clerks or something else above their station. Reading the Bible was necessary. Writing, beyond signing their own names, was not.

By the end of the 1700s, however, a schoolmaster was hired, and he made some changes. Writing was added to the daily lessons. Learning prayers and reciting the catechism were a large part of the curriculum, along with knitting (for boys), needlework and spinning (for girls, "in such manner as may enable them to make useful Servants") and singing. A drawing instructor was also hired, as well as a woman who taught the girls "Pencilling on Calico." (Calico is a kind of cloth.)

In addition to their lessons and work, the children were ordered to "be exercised in walking upright and strong without wadling," during a daily, supervised half-hour outing on the grounds. A drillmaster was later employed, and the boys spent half an hour after breakfast each day performing "parade ground activities" – marching and turning in unison, as they would later need to do in the army.

While Hannah Brown was a resident in the 1870s, lessons included dictation, reading, scripture and sums. She claims that although there were large maps hung "all round the school," they were never mentioned by the instructors, and she felt she knew nothing of geography. She also felt ignorant of grammar. Soon after her departure, tennis and croquet were introduced.

No sports equipment or toys were ever given to the girls. The boys, however, had bats and balls, tops and whips. They also had a sports day once a year; girls were kindly permitted into the boys' side to watch! Even when a library was eventually built, in 1836, it was "for the use of the older boys."

The level of everyday learning does not seem to have been terribly challenging, and very few students – paradoxically, usually girls – went on to

Thomas Coram disagreed with popular opinion on the matter of educating girls, and wrote that it

is an Evil amongst us here in England to think Girls having learning given them is not so very Material as for boys to have it. I think and say it is more Material, for Girls when they come to be Mothers will have the forming of their Children's lives and if their Mothers be good or Bad the Children Generally take after them so that Giving Girls a virtuous Education is a vast Advantage to their Posterity as well as to the Publick.

higher education. Most were content with what they got at the Hospital. "After all," said Amy, a former foundling, "we weren't going to be wonderful. We were mostly going into service" – meaning domestic service, working as servants in someone's home.

The Joy of Music

One area in which the Foundling Hospital excelled was musical instruction, thanks to the early patronage of George Handel. Hannah Brown described the contrast between strict Foundling discipline, and musical escape:

I never remember any punishment being inflicted on Sundays with that awful ruler which was kept in the head teacher's desk. Later, the beautiful music and singing in the Chapel at morning and afternoon service seemed to make the place a heaven . . . the Psalms were adorable and the grand old-fashioned chants intensified the beautiful language. The anthems and oratorios were a joy to take part in.

All children became members of the choir at the age of nine, and were coached two hours a week in performing the Foundling hymns and anthems. As well as "The Foundling Hospital Anthem," Handel wrote the often-sung "Angels ever Bright and Fair," and "How beautiful are the feet of them that preach the Gospel of Peace." Another favourite was this version of Psalm 51:

Wash off my foul offence
And cleanse me from my Sin;
For I confess my crime, and see
How great my Guilt has been.

The governors realized that the choir singing in chapel on Sunday mornings could attract Londoners and increase donations to the collection plate. The choice of music seems aimed at recognizing the low birth and dependent gratitude of the singers – likely a strategy to flatter benefactors and encourage further generosity.

A boys' band was established in 1837, and became quite renowned for its ability. Boys were selected to play instruments according to the size of their hands or lips, rather than whether they had any musical ability or even interest. One foundling, named John, explained:

So you just went along and saw Mr. Owen. He was a captain in some regiment. Quite a nice bloke. And he'd look at your hands and if you had little stubby fingers, you were a cornet player. If they were nice and long, you were a clarinet player or some other instrument.

The novelist Charles Dickens described his encounter with the band during a tour of the Foundling in 1853:

These young musicians, about thirty in number, now made their appearance, and commenced the performance of some difficult Italian music, executed with so much precision and spirit as amply to justify the expressions of commendation and surprise, which we found in letters addressed to their music-master by that admirable artist, Signor Costa, and by Mr. Godfrey, one of the bandmasters of the Household troops.

(For more on Charles Dickens, see the end of this chapter.)
Most of the boys who played in the Foundling band went on to have musical careers – usually with the army, in regimental bands. (Arthur Jocelyn had nice long fingers. He played the clarinet and saxophone, and joined the army's North Staffordshire Regiment when he was fifteen.)

Girls at choir practice. For many young children Sunday mornings seemed long.
One foundling remembers being at Sunday service when "every small bullet head
bent forward and touched the wooden rail in front, and every spotless apron covered
every spotless face, and every girl too leant forward, face in apron, apparently to pray
for God's blessing on humanity in general and foundlings in particular."

Learning Labour

❧

The schoolroom was not the only place for learning. For much of the
Hospital's life, there was greater emphasis on industry than on academic and
artistic lessons. The governors felt that training for future jobs was an essential
part of the children's education, beginning when they first returned from
their foster homes in the country.

Many different jobs occupied the foundlings over the years. Some jobs contributed to the Hospital itself, such as manufacturing uniforms, while others
supposedly prepared the children to be members of the nation's workforce.

Despite the old-fashioned pinafores and bonnets, this photo was likely taken in the 1920s or 1930s. The children may have posed especially for it; even then, it was most unusual for boys and girls to sit together.

Daily chores, particularly for the girls, taught the basic duties of a domestic servant; scrubbing floors, doing endless laundry, assisting the cooks with meals and washing the dishes were all part of the schedule, along with the needle skills of knitting, spinning, sewing and darning.

Many of the work duties involved making various sorts of handicrafts; the specific items changed over the years as the committee noted what might be useful or popular, from cloth to rope to straw hats. The committee was interested not only in saving money by not spending it on things that could be produced by the foundlings, but also in making money, however little, from the children's creations.

Some paid needlework was brought in from outside, but most projects were part of an ongoing in-house industry. The manufacture of twine and fishing nets, and later of garters and purses, was so popular that the committee recommended that a studio shop be set up where customers could watch the children at their work, and could be inspired to buy more. There were tradesmen in the nearby Covent Garden market who claimed to sell "foundling made purses," but in truth the genuine articles could only be purchased from the matron.

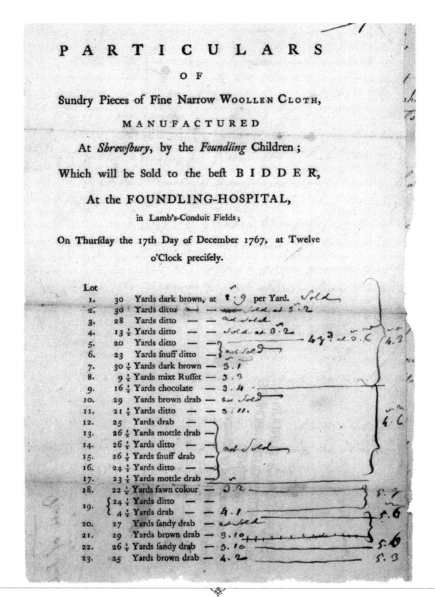

PARTICULARS

OF

Sundry Pieces of Fine Narrow WOOLLEN CLOTH,

MANUFACTURED

At *Shrewsbury*, by the *Foundling* Children;

Which will be Sold to the beft B I D D E R,

At the FOUNDLING-HOSPITAL,

in Lamb's-Conduit Fields;

On Thurſday the 17th Day of December 1767, at Twelve o'Clock precifely.

Lot			
1.	30	Yards dark brown, at 9 per Yard.	Sold
2.	30	Yards ditto	Sold at 3.2
3.	28	Yards ditto	not Sold
4.	13½	Yards ditto	Sold at 3.2
5.	20	Yards ditto	
6.	23	Yards fnuff ditto	not Sold
7.	30½	Yards dark brown	3.1
8.	9½	Yards mixt Ruffet	3.3
9.	16½	Yards chocolate	3.4
10.	29	Yards brown drab	not Sold
11.	21½	Yards ditto	3.11
12.	25	Yards drab	
13.	26½	Yards mottle drab	
14.	26½	Yards ditto	not Sold
15.	26¼	Yards fnuff drab	
16.	24½	Yards ditto	
17.	23½	Yards mottle drab	
18.	22½	Yards fawn colour	3.2
19.	24½ Yards ditto		
	4½ Yards drab	4.1	
20.	27	Yards fandy drab	not Sold
21.	29	Yards brown drab	3.10
22.	26½	Yards fandy drab	3.10
23.	25	Yards brown drab	4.2

❧

During the first few decades, older children were usefully employed in making cloth such as the woollen lengths listed here. Their product was prized highly enough that on December 7, 1760, a group of artists at the Turk's Head Tavern chose to wear a uniform and agreed "to appear next 5th November at the Artists Feast at the Foundling Hospital in Lamb's Conduit Fields, in a suit of clothes manufactured by the Children of the Hospital. . . ." Committee minutes for 1767 note that a young man "living at the Three Tun Tavern in the field adjoining this Hospital" was given "a complete suit of clothes made of the Hospital Cloth for his service in giving information of the Fire that broke out in the Messenger's room last Thursday evening."

The Mills

"The mills" were factories where fabric was produced in large quantities. The very name struck fear into the hearts of many. The workers, frequently children, laboured at tedious, repetitive tasks for twelve or fourteen hours a day. Often the air was thick with lint, and the noise was unbearable.

But because it could be difficult to find dozens of apprenticeship positions, the Foundling Hospital occasionally sent children to work in these miserable sweatshops. The first time this happened, in 1777, twenty-five girls were sent to a mill in Stockport, in northern England. It turned out, however, that they were barely clothed, and were only used to tie broken silk thread onto bobbins; they were not being trained in any useful occupation.

The governors did not repeat the experiment until nearly twenty years later, when they agreed to provide twenty-five boys and girls, aged six to fourteen, to the Cuckney Mills in Nottinghamshire, also in the north, for seven years of labour. The owners of the mill promised to teach the children reading, writing and arithmetic, and to send them to church every Sunday. Uniforms "of good quality" were issued and the diet consisted of meat pies, suet puddings and brown bread. Also pledged was that the boys were "to be Educated and Employed entirely separate and apart from the Females."

The arrangement seemed to succeed, until the company went bankrupt with no warning and its four hundred child employees were abandoned to the parish, which could not, of course, look after them. The Hospital swooped in to rescue its foundlings, but the other children were bundled into carts and taken to workhouses in London.

Workhouses were begun in 1834 as places to put poor people who had nowhere else to go. Families were separated – husband from wife, parents from children – and they were all fed on thin gruel and expected to toil many hours each day at mindless or backbreaking jobs. The "inmates" were allowed visitors only under supervision, and if they moved out of the workhouse, they had to leave the parish as well, so as never to be a burden again. Most people would do anything to avoid ending up in the workhouse.

Working Children

These days, we have strict laws about when and how children are allowed to work outside the home, to protect their health and safety, and save their energy for school. In earlier centuries, though, children often had to work — as they still do today in some countries — to keep the family from starving. From the age of six or seven, they would be expected to add a few pence to the family income. For example, children were useful underground, in the mining pits, to open the trapdoors providing ventilation, or to push and haul carts to and from the bottom of the mine shaft. A day's work meant twelve or more silent hours in pitch dark. There were also thousands of homeless children living in the streets of London, some in groups and some completely on their own. The competition among beggars often meant that children were mutilated — purposely blinded or made lame — so that people would pity them more. There was no law enforcing school attendance until 1880, and the total average length of time a poor child spent in school was about eighteen months.

Here are some of the jobs that children ended up doing.

Mudlark, or river scavenger

These children scoured the banks and bed of the River Thames at low tide. They were filthy and smelly, but persistent and sometimes lucky. Their main findings were lumps of coal, fallen from barges, that could be used for fuel. They also looked for coins, firewood, glass or stone bottles, bits of hardware and anything else that might be sold for a penny or two.

> They pounce on little knobs of coal . . .; lovingly coil up limp lengths of sodden rope that look like drowned, putrefying snakes; wrangle over broken bones . . .; make prize of bits of wood . . .; exult over a rusty iron bolt or lock, and can scarce believe their delighted eyes when their grubby hands have fished up half a dozen . . . copper nails.

Crossing sweeper

It was usually boys who claimed their "personal crossing" and did this dangerous job of scurrying into the road ahead of rich folk — dashing between horses and horse-drawn carriages before there were traffic lights or stop signs

Charles Dickens portrayed a crossing sweeper in his novel Bleak House: *"Jo sweeps his crossing all day. . . . He knows that it's hard to keep the mud off the crossing in dirty weather, and harder still to live by doing it."*

– to brush mud and manure out of the way. If they were lucky, they were rewarded with some tiny coin.

Climbing boy or chimney sweep (also known as a "chummy")

Before the days of gas and electricity, houses were heated with stoves and fireplaces, and chimneys soon became blocked by soot that had to be swept out. The smallest boys, beginning at age four or five, were the most desirable sweeps because they could wedge their bodies up narrow chimneys, poking a broom above them to disperse the clogs of filthy soot. In Dickens' novel *Oliver Twist*, the heartless Gamfield defends his treatment of the sweeps he employs:

> "Young boys have been smothered in chimneys before now," said another gentleman.
>
> "That's acause they damped the straw afore they lit it in the chimbley to make 'em come down agin," said Gamfield; "that's all smoke, and no blaze; vereas smoke ain't o' no use at all in making a boy come down, for it only sinds him to sleep, and that's wot he likes. Boys is wery obstinit, and wery lazy, gen'lmen, and there's nothink like a good hot blaze to make 'em come down vith a run. It's humane too, gen'l-men, acause, even if they've stuck in the chimbley, roasting their feet makes 'em struggle to hextricate theirselves."

Chimney sweeping was perhaps the most dangerous job, as the bad air and tight spaces often resulted in lung diseases, testicular cancer or death by suffocation. The boys were usually "owned" by someone who worked them hard and fed them little, in a effort to keep them small enough to do the job.

Watercress (or matches or bootlaces or oranges) girl

Very small children stood on corners or wandered the streets trying to sell their scant supply of cheap wares. Profits from yesterday – a penny or two – would pay for today's merchandise, whether that meant bunches of violets and watercress or a few sticks of wood or matches. Bad weather, of course, meant bad business.

Hans Christian Andersen described the plight of a little match girl: "In a corner, between two houses, one of which projected beyond the other, she sank down and huddled herself together. She had drawn her little feet under her, but she could not keep off the cold; and she dared not go home, for she had sold no matches, and could not take home even a penny of money. Her father would certainly beat her. . . ."

Like William Hogarth, Dickens spent a year of his childhood in a debtors' prison — the famous Marshalsea, which he later used as a setting in his novel Little Dorrit. *Dickens' father had overspent his income, giving extravagant parties, and was arrested for not paying his bills. Young Charles was punished for his father's mistakes; he was sent to work in a boot-blacking factory, gluing labels on bottles of boot polish for six shillings a week. He never forgot this episode of hardship, and it inspired his literary outspokenness on behalf of the poor and downtrodden.*

Charles Dickens

Charles Dickens created some of the most famous orphans in English literature: Little Nell, Pip, David Copperfield and Oliver Twist. He lived in London about a hundred years after Captain Coram died. His house was only a few blocks from the Foundling Hospital, and he was a frequent visitor at the Sunday chapel services.

Dickens wrote many wonderful novels, often featuring characters from the lowliest circles of society: thieves and beggars, misfits and foundlings. He also wrote hundreds of newspaper stories and articles, commenting on society in all its many guises. In 1853 he wrote an article for a magazine called *Household Words*. It was entitled "Received, a Blank Child," and was a profile of the Foundling Hospital.

"This home of the blank children is by no means a blank place . . .," he says, and goes on to describe the grounds, including an "incredible fishpond," the "commodious roomy comfortable building," the impressive art collection and the "noble organ" donated by Handel. Then he relates the arrival of two foundlings:

One was a boy; the other a girl. A parchment ticket inscribed [with] the figures 20,563 was sewn upon the shoulder-strap of the male infant and a similar ticket was attached to the female infant, denoting that she was 20,564 – so numerous were the babies who had been there before them.

It is a long and favourable report, with this statement near the end:

Such is the home of the blank children, where they are trained out of their blank state to be useful entities in life. It is rich, and it is likely enough that it has its blemishes . . . but from what we have seen of this establishment we have derived much satisfaction, and the good that is in it seems to have grown with its growth.

Why are orphans so popular in books and movies? In reality it is a horrible thought that a child might be abandoned, without the love and protection of parents. But authors have discovered that a child who faces the world alone, with bravery and cleverness, is an appealing character to readers of all ages. Think of Jane Eyre, Oliver Twist, Little Nell, Huck Finn, Anne of Green Gables, Molly Moon and, of course, Harry Potter.

CHAPTER FIVE

Illness and Other Woes

rom their first hour at the Foundling, babies and children received some of the finest medical care in London. Throughout the years a series of prominent doctors donated regular visits to the Hospital, and treated a wide range of illness and injury, including the most common ailments, such as smallpox, "the Itch," "the Fever," scrofula (a form of tuberculosis) and scorbutic eruptions (sores related to scurvy).

Aside from the benevolence of caring for children in need, the foundlings allowed doctors a unique opportunity. Medical science was just beginning to understand that "controlled studies" – set up to avoid random factors that might affect the results – could provide essential information for developing new treatments. At the Foundling they had a large number of children raised in similar circumstances on the same diet – an ideal situation for comparing the results of different treatments. More than one medical innovation was introduced at the Hospital.

All this attention was good for the foundlings, too. During an era when the general public was battling numerous threatening diseases, these children usually survived at a better rate than their peers outside the gates.

When the Hospital opened, Dr. Richard Mead – a favourite of the king, and one of the original governors of the Foundling – examined some of the first babies.

Dr. Mead liked to sit in a coffeehouse and issue prescriptions for patients he had never seen, trusting his knowledge of how to treat the symptoms reported to him. He tended personally to the very rich, however, and earned a lot of money. He rode in a gilded carriage drawn by six horses, with two footmen running alongside. His early medical studies included working with poisonous snakes. In his later work, he strived to conquer smallpox.

He was generous with his skills when it came to the poor and destitute, and continued his attachment to the Foundling for many years. Although germs had not yet been discovered and nobody knew how diseases were spread, he believed that fresh air contributed to good health. His theory prompted the governors to send sickly children to the countryside to recover.

Dr. William Cadogan became the Foundling Hospital physician in 1754, and began by writing the governors a lengthy letter putting forth what were, at the time, extraordinary ideas:

> The Foundlings under the Care of the Hospital, I presume, will be bred in a very plain, simple Manner: They will therefore infallibly have the more Health, Beauty, Strength, and Spirits; I might add Understanding too, as all the Faculties of the Mind are well known to depend upon the Organs of the Body; so that when these are in good Order, the thinking Part is most alert and active. . . .

Dr. Cadogan published a book on the care of infants, arguing that breast-fed babies were more likely to stay healthy, and even alive, than those who were "dry" nursed. He also challenged the accepted belief that babies should be kept hot and swaddled (tightly wrapped):

besides the Mischief arising from the Weight and Heat of these Swaddling-cloaths, they are put on so tight, and the Child is so cramp'd by them, that its Bowels have not room, nor the Limbs any Liberty, to act and exert themselves in the free easy manner they ought. This is a very hurtful Circumstance; for Limbs that are not used will never be strong, and such tender Bodies cannot bear much Pressure. . . .

He went on to recommend that babies wear loose-fitting flannel gowns, and reminded the reader that "shoes and stockings are very needless Incumbrances. . . ."

The Foundling Hospital nurses seem to have disregarded Dr. Cadogan's theories on swaddling. However, the committee did decide that while children were being fostered in the country, they should go barefoot "to make them healthy and hardy."

Dr. Cadogan's recipe for pap — the formula fed to newborns — was only partially followed. His suggestion of making it by mixing bread with milk instead of water was ignored, but the nurses agreed to stop adding sugar, butter or a "calming" dose of wine!

The Dreaded Pox

During the Hospital's first hundred years, smallpox was widespread in the city of London. The disease killed nearly a quarter of the children who got it, and often wiped out entire families. Smallpox caused the skin to erupt in hundreds of hideous pustules that left serious scars on those lucky enough to survive. For the foundlings, living in such close quarters, this highly infectious virus posed a terrible risk.

As early as the 1720s, some doctors believed that smallpox could be prevented by inoculation – that is, by inserting a small amount of fluid from a smallpox pustule into a healthy person. The body's immune system built a defence against the mild infection, making the person less likely to get ill if he or she was later exposed again.

Inoculation for smallpox had been introduced into Britain in 1718 by Lady Mary Wortley Montagu, wife of the British ambassador to Turkey.

The Montagus arrived in Turkey in 1717 and Lady Montagu wrote dozens of letters about her travels. In one she described what was to her a remarkable procedure:

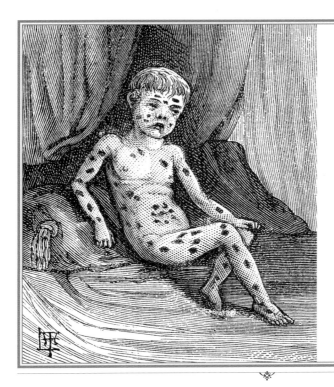

In 1830, almost half the funerals in London were for children under ten years old — and many had died of smallpox. Those who survived were often badly scarred.

The small-pox, so fatal, and so general amongst us, is here entirely harmless, by the invention of engrafting, which is the term they give it. There is a set of old women, who make it their business to perform the operation. . . . the old woman comes with a nut-shell full of the matter of the best sort of small-pox, and asks what vein you please to have opened. She immediately rips open that you offer to her, with a large needle (which gives you no more pain than a common scratch) and puts into the vein as much matter as can lie upon the head of her nee-dle, and after that, binds up the little wound with a hollow bit of shell, and in this manner opens four or five veins. . . . The children or young patients play together all the rest of the day, and are in perfect health to the eighth. Then the fever begins to seize them, and they keep their beds two days, very seldom three. They have very rarely above twenty or thirty [pustules] in their faces, which never mark, and in eight days time they are as well as before their illness. . . . There is no example of any one that has died in it, and you may believe I am well satisfied of the safety of this experiment, since I intend to try it on my dear little son. I am patriot enough to take the pains to bring this useful invention into fashion in England . . .

Lady Montagu took a personal interest in smallpox. Her brother had died of it, and she herself had suffered the disease back in England, resulting in a terribly scarred face and the loss of her "very fine eyelashes." The painter of this portrait was considerate enough to ignore the defects left by the disease.

Thanks in part to her efforts, inoculation was soon recognized in England as a life-saving procedure.

While the average death rate of people with smallpox was one in six, inoculation diminished the risk of death to one in fifty. With variations in injection technique and other treatments, this ratio improved over the next forty years to one death in five hundred cases.

Inoculations were first performed at the Foundling Hospital in 1744, with the committee meeting in a nearby tavern to avoid any contact with contagious children. Later, they rented a house in Leather Lane, to assure themselves of a pox-free place to gather.

By 1767, Sir William Watson was the doctor at the Foundling, and he was most interested in perfecting the method of inoculation. His approach would be considered normal scientific practice today, but back then it was revolutionary. In carefully documented experiments, he tested dozens of foundlings to determine the best source of smallpox fluid – an early pustule? A mature pock? – and whether other steps of preparation were helpful. Dr. Watson's studies laid the groundwork for many later advances.

Around 1800, Dr. Edward Jenner developed a different kind of inoculation, using fluid from cattle with cowpox, a disease similar to smallpox but safer for people. The usually forward-thinking governors of the Foundling resisted Dr. Jenner's breakthrough and for a couple of years continued to inoculate the children with smallpox. Not until cowpox vaccine was a proven worldwide success, a few years later, did the foundlings get Dr. Jenner's vaccine as a matter of course.

Other Health Measures

The governors of the Foundling Hospital were tireless in their efforts to protect the children, and a great range of precautions were taken through the years, against infections, infestations of parasites and other health hazards.

Mr. George Bridges was hired in 1756 to destroy bed "buggs" at threepence per bed per year. His irresistible terms were "No cure, no money."

In 1773 it was decided that "the Clothes of such children suffering from the Itch be baked in the Oven after the Bread is drawn," and that the apothecary (pharmacist) was "to see that the clothes be delivered to the Steward who is to take care that the Baker put them into the Oven for an hour."

Any clothes worn by infected children were to be "cast-off clothes and to be burnt after their cure."

In August of 1773, a boy was killed as the result of sliding on the banisters. The committee ordered an "Iron Rail to be placed 12 inches above the present wooden Banister, 3 spikes in every flight."

A report in 1804 noted that placing "The Heads of the Beds under the Windows . . . may hurt the hearing and sight of the children," with no explanation as to why this might be so.

In July 1807, a person was hired to keep the Hospital free of rats – which carried fleas, which might carry disease – for three guineas each year.

Pills and Potions

Although medical drugs as we know them were nearly non-existent in the 1800s, a great many supposed remedies were used. Some worked, some did not, and some were actually harmful. Hospital records note, for example, that to purge (empty) the bowels of an infant

Emma Brownlow King's painting The Sick Room *probably makes the infirmary look a little nicer than it really was. Note that the boy on the left has his arm in a sling. Doctors did not yet understand germs; today we would not want small children rubbing their hands on a hospital floor!*

The general practice of the Matron is to use Sirrup of Violets or of Roses with oil of sweet Almonds, a Tea-Spoonful of small Quantity to cleanse its Body; and if the Child is very tender, it is recommended that a little simple Cinnamon water be mixed.

The records also note that "The Swelled Bellies of Children will usually give way to a little Rhubarb and Anniseed in small doses once a day," and that "Children in the Country about Autumn are subject to a kind of Cholic which will kill Them in a few hours; And for which nothing is so proper as a good warm Clyster of fat meat with a spoonful of Salt. . . ."

Despite the lack of modern medicines, some combination of care and luck allowed the matron to report, in July 1805, that "only one child, a boy, [has] died since Christmas. Not a girl [has] been buried out of the house since April twelve months."

Punishment and Bullying

Although physical punishment was an accepted form of discipline, it was often overused by those staff members who were bullies by nature. From the victim's point of view, there was not much difference between being beaten by a matron and being shoved about by a bigger boy in the dormitory. Almost all foundling recollections tell us that both kinds of bullying happened often.

There were many complaints about adults who misused their authority, according to Hannah Brown – ranging from a schoolmistress who addressed her pupils as "Children of Shame" to a seamstress (known as Quacker because of her voice) who was particularly vicious in her punishments. Quacker's favourite weapon was a hoopstick – a stick used to roll a hoop, in play – and the marks of her beatings could often be seen across the girls' shoulders at bath time. The visiting doctor did not approve of this sort of discipline, but if a girl had the bad luck to have her bruises noticed by the doctor – leading him to scold the seamstress – the girl would get an extra beating next time.

The children were punished for a variety of crimes, including swearing, gambling, breaking windows, playing with the clock pendulum, sliding on the banisters, speaking during silent times, not knowing the answer when called upon in class, failing to look "smart" on the parade ground, begging from visitors and swiping fruit from the garden.

The worst thing a girl could do was to discuss her period:

> The school seems to have wanted changing bodies and sexuality to be kept a secret. Girls were punished severely if they shared information about menstruation, for instance. You got the cane and your name in the Black Book. . . . We thought there was something dreadfully wrong with us.

Hannah Brown was put in solitary confinement up in a tower called the Cat's Garret for a full weekend, as punishment for teasing a kitchen maid; she was given bread and water twice a day and a blanket to sleep on. One eight-year-old boy spent a week alone before it was judged that he sufficiently repented.

Charles Nalden, who lived in the Hospital from 1913, says,

My own generation, mercifully, was spared the terrifying form of punishment meted out to our erring 18th century counterparts, girls and boys alike, when the recess on the north side of the organ was fitted up as a place of solitary confinement. Children incarcerated in this airless Dark Room were restricted to a diet of bread and water. It was put into operation shortly following the publication of a pamphlet extolling the benefits of solitary confinement, the brainchild of that otherwise humanitarian-philanthropical governor, Jonas Hanway.

Sometimes, the older foundlings seemed to be in cahoots with the matrons. Hannah Brown described two examples of their bullying:

As we were not able to keep awake [in chapel], the big girls would thump us in the back every time we nodded, and punish us the next day.

Two bigger girls were placed at the side of the gallery with pencils and papers, writing down names of fidgety foundlings. The children were punished for fidgeting in chapel, including "'moving their heads from side to side.'"

Hannah also remembered that the monitors, or bigger girls, liked to torment the little ones when teachers were absent, by pushing them into the "Dark Hole" beneath the gallery seats. Other girls were commanded to jump up and down on the gallery, making a thundering noise to terrify the prisoners beneath. Shouted cries of "Thieves are coming! Thieves are coming!" threatened the most dreaded of all monsters.

Bullies were still in power a century later. Ken Budden recalled:

My most vivid memories [are of] the physical abuse we suffered at the hands of the bigger boys. We called them Big Chaps but they were, in fact, Monitors. We were repeatedly beaten with cricket stumps, canes, and, I well remember, with a Wellington boot across the stomach. We were kicked between our open legs, commonly known then as "Nourishment Divine."

Each Monitor had "Payers up," which meant that any food the Monitor wanted, you HAD to give him for fear of getting a beating. A Monitor may have had as many as 10–12 "Payers up." Chocolate or sweets, in VERY short supply because of the war, were immediately handed over.

Jonas Hanway, a trader during the eighteenth century, travelled as far away as Russia and Persia. Once he was home in England again, he wrote about his adventures, including an attack by pirates, and made quite a name for himself. He became an opinionated social activist, outspoken on behalf of chimney sweeps, unwed mothers, apprentice seamen and babies dying in the workhouses.

He was also a conscientious governor of the Foundling Hospital, and a member of the subcommittee that met every week. He discovered that certain parishes were hiding the number of children in their care who died from neglect and starvation, and his relentless criticism resulted in Parliament passing two bills that forced improvements. The first insisted on careful record-keeping of the children living and dying in workhouses. The second – nicknamed the Hanway Act – compelled parish officials to turn illegitimate children over to the Foundling Hospital, and to pay a set amount toward their support.

Hanway published his opinions, on everything from the dangers of drinking tea to the advantages of musical amusements and the risks of caring for deserted children, in a series of articles. Though he was often a thoughtful do-gooder, he had troubling views about the values of solitary confinement, expressed in an influential essay: "Solitude in Imprisonment, With proper profitable Labour And a Spare Diet, The most humane and effectual Means of bringing Malefactors . . . to a right Sense of their Condition. . . ."

Jonas Hanway was devoted to correcting social wrongs, but he is perhaps remembered most for discovering an invention during his travels and introducing it into his native country. Hanway was the first person in London to use an umbrella! Although he was mocked for several years because of it, his bizarre contraption is now the symbol of a classic Englishman.

At the time it seemed like the norm, we knew no other life, we could not compare, and eventually we learned to bear the pain and not cry. AND of course, we DID NOT squeal. I vividly remember one boy who did tell a master [teacher], and the monitor concerned made us hold the boy about two feet off the floor, spreadeagled, face down, and he was beaten with a cricket stump mercilessly.

In the dining hall, girls and boys were originally separated, but in the 1940s a new headmaster changed the rules and let them sit together. Every bit of food had to be eaten, or the children were sent back to their seats to finish up. "I suppose I was a bit of a smartie," says Ken Budden. "I would put the food in my hand under the plate and then toss it into a garbage bin after stacking my plate."

In an eerie echo of Hannah Brown's report a hundred years earlier, Ken goes on to say:

His backside was literally black and blue, and he was warned NOT to let a master see it on bathnight. I remember the boy FACING the master in the bathroom . . . to avoid being seen, and thankfully for the boy, he managed to hide the bruises. HAD he been seen, he would have had another beating. All boys who were in my age group were subject to these beatings by the "big chaps," and I know several friends who will confirm this. . . .

The Masters were equally as brutal as the Monitors, I recall 4 boys getting caught for stealing from a shop in Berkhamsted, just very minor items such as a comic or some sweets, and the whole school was

Young Ken Budden leads the girls in a windy "crocodile walk," in not the best
weather for bonnets. Ken now says that he must have been "in disgrace"
that day – the only reason a boy might be seen walking with girls.

assembled. Each boy received 24 strokes of the cane. Needless to say
they never stole again, and from that a lesson should be learned for
today's generation.

Chava Cohen, another foundling during the 1940s, has distressing recollections of the nurses: "No one to say good morning to. No one to say good
night to. Just bam bam bam bam. That's abuse. I can name girls who were
beaten on a daily basis." She remembers one girl who was "stood up against
the dining room wall and smacked so hard that blood came out of her nose."

It seems that deep friendships were rare among the foundlings. Perhaps
this was because they were each protecting what little privacy they had.
Perhaps it was because, as one ex-foundling explains, "We were all doing the
same thing. There was no excitement. There was nothing to talk about. . . ."
But Ken Budden has a different memory:

I think one of the biggest things we learned at the home was a wonderful sense of comradeship. We never "ratted" on anyone, possibly because we were too scared to report the beatings from the "big chaps," so a great camaraderie was formed between us.

People who live in a closed society gradually develop their own slang. The foundlings were no exception. One word that was used for at least a hundred years was *glishing*, meaning wanting something very much, or revelling in having it. "Glishing jolly thick" meant yearning almost beyond description. Other terms were:

atching up	pretending
think-tale	proud
yarders	toilet paper
top deckers	underpants showing above one's shorts
fishing	picking one's nose
natchit	food
feeling bate	feeling stupid
feeling monk	feeling miserable
dob up	hand over food to a bully

CHAPTER SIX

Apprenticeship and Domestic Service

 or most of the foundlings, who had been sheltered for their whole lives, it was a moment of huge importance to step into the world as an apprentice or domestic servant. Although the "graduate" would likely be accompanied on that first journey to a new home, he or she would soon be expected to navigate the streets of London alone.

During the eighteenth and nineteenth centuries, the city held unimagined sights and smells: clattering coaches and horses; street vendors selling wares the foundlings might never have seen before, such as gin or abundant flowers or whole sides of beef abuzz with flies. The foundlings had never used money, bartered with tradesmen or had reason to think about pickpockets. There were beggars, prostitutes and animals roaming the cobblestones, mud and sewage sloshing in the gutters, profanity, fighting and noise filling the air. After the sedate order within the walls of the Hospital, life outside must have been nearly overwhelming.

The children form orderly ranks, like soldiers, for official inspection.
Eyes front! Chin up! Toes out!

Terms of Employment

Although there were changes and challenges to the governors' apprenticeship policy through the years, the general formula was that children were placed as apprentices or servants upon turning fourteen; the governors would pay an annual fee to the master (employer) for a set number of years (usually five to seven) and would continue to show interest and even provide financial support until the young person came of age at twenty-one.

In the dozen years after the first foundlings reached the age of apprenticeship, an average of eighteen children were placed in employment each year. (Only this few out of hundreds in a given year, prior to General Reception, had survived this long!) The numbers began to jump in 1760, when there were forty-two "graduating" foundlings. In 1765, there were 253. By 1769 there were 1,430 young people all needing jobs. This was a result of those years of General Reception, when there was no limit to the number of babies accepted. It was difficult to find positions for so many children at once; it was impossible to investigate properly whether each master was a good one, and there was little time for follow-up visits or inspections. A social worker today normally has an average of 25 cases to take care of. The governors of the Foundling Hospital were depending on about a dozen people to keep track of 4,000 apprentices – or one worker for over 300 apprentices!

This sometimes resulted in serious trouble. There were many complaints about masters mistreating their apprentices: starving them, overworking them, underclothing them, not teaching them the promised trade, even beating them – or worse.

James Brownrigg, a painter in Fetter Lane, had a wife who abused a foundling named Mary Jones by whipping her and dunking her head repeatedly in a pail of water. Mary ran away, straight back to the Foundling Hospital, and the governors quickly found her a new position. But two years later Mrs. Brownrigg killed another apprentice, an eleven-year-old girl she had hired from a parish home. The examining doctor said the child was "all one wound from her head to her toes."

Another girl, Jemima Dixon, was killed by a weaver named William Butterworth. At the murder trial, an eyewitness reported that Jemima had been starved, slapped and beaten with a weaver's shuttle, and that Butterworth had "punch'd or kick'd her on the Belly with his foot and broke her Belly. . . ."

After this sad incident, the governors tried harder to be vigilant about where the children went and how they fared when they got there. And of course there were some apprentices who did not fulfill the requirements of the job, who were lazy or uncooperative. The masters and mistresses sent "report cards" to the Hospital each year, assessing the performance of their apprentices.

Before leaving the Foundling Hospital, all apprentices were given a Bible, a suit of clothing and a letter of strict direction:

You are placed out Apprentice by the Governors of this Hospital. You were taken into it very young, quite helpless, forsaken, poor and deserted. Out of Charity you have been fed, clothed and instructed; which many have wanted.

You have been taught to fear God; to love him, to be honest, careful, laborious and diligent. As you hope for Success in this World, and Happiness in the next, you are to be mindful of what has been taught you. You are to behave honestly, justly, soberly, and carefully, in every

We don't know what kind of work Susannah Cartwright was doing, but it seems her honesty did not make up for her disobedience; in this annual report card her mistress begs to be relieved of her, "and that soon"!

thing, to every body, and especially towards your Master and his Family; and to execute all lawful commands with Industry, Cheerfulness, and good Manners.

You may find many temptations to do wickedly, when you are in the world; but by all means fly from them. Always speak the Truth. Though you may have done a wrong thing, you will, by sincere Confession, more easily obtain Forgiveness, than if by an obstinate Lie you make the fault the greater, and thereby deserve a far greater Punishment. Lying is the beginning of everything that is bad; and a Person used to it is never believed, esteemed or trusted.

Be not ashamed that you were bred in this Hospital. Own it; and say, that it was through the good Providence of Almighty God, that you were taken Care of. Bless him for it.

Be constant in your Prayers, and going to Church; and avoid Gaming, Swearing, and all evil Discourses. By this means the Blessing of God will follow your honest Labours, and you may be happy; otherwise you will bring upon yourself Misery, Shame, and Want.

Note. At Easter of every year, upon producing a testimonial of good conduct for the previous twelve months to the satisfaction of the Committee, you will receive a pecuniary reward proportioned to the length of time you have been apprenticed; and, at the termination of your Apprenticeship, upon producing a like testimonial for the whole term thereof, the further sum of Five Guineas, or such a smaller sum as the Committee shall consider you entitled to.

This plate is from a series of Hogarth engravings titled Idleness and Industry.
It shows a wicked master threatening to beat his young apprentices,
who are struggling to weave fabric on a loom. The device in front is
a spinning wheel, for turning fibres into thread.

Of course, young children had more hope of success if they were placed in work that suited their abilities. In December 1772, the committee decided to "take into Consideration the propriety of Enquiring into the different Geniuses, Character and Disposition of the children in this Hospital, in Order to endeavour to form them for those Occupations they may be most proper for." The schoolmaster and schoolmistresses were ordered to give an account of the children each month with some suggestion of how they might eventually be placed. Here is the first list from the schoolmaster:

1 John Printer (blind boy) Organist
3 Taylors
11 Darners
50 Knitters
2 Garden boys
1 Baker
1 Messenger
20 Quite Young there is no forming any judgment of their dispositions

The Schoolmistresses' report was:

17 Shirt and Shift Menders
5 Darners
17 Knitters
12 Spinning
13 Coat Making and several young children not capable of anything.

In a sample year, boys were apprenticed as follows:	3 to hairdressers
	2 to hair manufacturers [wig-makers]
16 to tailors	1 to a silversmith
16 to boot and shoe makers	2 to opticians
7 to fishermen	1 to a tin-plate worker
4 to cabinetmakers	1 to a weaver
3 to linen drapers	2 to law writers
2 to confectioners	1 to a watchmaker
2 to bakers	4 as domestic servants
2 to gold beaters	

The chapel embodied the Hospital's emphasis on music and religion. Note the magnificent organ in the back, donated by Handel. While Captain Coram's body rested beneath the chapel, the children could be less than reverent about their benefactor. Hannah Brown remembered one ghost story handed down for generations, insisting that "in the stone catacombs below the Chapel, Captain Coram's coffin was rotting away with age . . . it was partly open, and one hand was hanging out!"

Servant Life

During the 1800s more girls and women were working in England as servants than at any other job. Thousands of foundlings were among them, trained to be housemaids or nursemaids through their daily chores, the attention paid to their sewing skills and their duties in caring for the younger children. Their patchy education in other areas was not seen as a problem. But girls who had grown up gazing at great works of art and singing exquisite music every Sunday probably found the change to drudgery and loneliness a difficult one.

Foundling girls who became servants exchanged one uniform for another, and went from the strict school regimen to a life of relentless toil. No wonder these young women, photographed in 1886, had nothing to smile about.

Like the boys, they were prepared for their departure with new clothes, a Bible and a letter. The older girls going into service stitched their own clothes for the occasion, but with firm guidance. Hannah Brown didn't think much of the outfit. She said they

wore long dresses devoid of cut or shape, which made the wearer look as though she had no "figure" at all. The legs were encased in white stockings and elastic-sided boots. In addition to all this, a hair-net. . . .

For Hannah, being a servant meant fifteen hours a day of hard work. On her very first day, though, she encountered something new. Entering the nursery in the big house, she was greeted by a *dog* – an animal she had never met before!

Life as a domestic servant was likely much harder than life as a foundling. A maid's bedroom was usually in the basement or attic of the house, icy in winter and sweltering in summer. The workday for a housemaid generally began at six in the morning and finished around ten o'clock at night. The chores included lugging coal and warmed water up several flights of stairs, cleaning fireplace grates, laying and lighting fires, making and serving meals, scrubbing pots and doing mountains of laundry by hand. In many households there were only one or two other young servants, and there were usually firm rules against meeting friends elsewhere. Many employers did not permit their housemaids to have boyfriends.

No wonder runaway servant girls were often returned by the police to the Foundling Hospital.

The "Other" Foundlings

Despite the work and lack of freedom, most servants and apprentices could count their blessings. Although they had no family to help them, they had a safe home, decent clothes and regular meals. Many Londoners of the time had less.

Of course, not all foundlings followed the usual pattern. During the General Reception years in particular, scores of babies delivered to the Hospital were mentally handicapped, crippled, severely epileptic, blind or disabled in some other way. As there were not yet effective treatments for any of these afflictions, those children needed special care all their lives.

Interestingly, there were several blind children who grew up to be musically gifted. Special lessons were arranged for them, on the harpsichord and organ. As for Mercy Draper, who sang so beautifully, the governors decided that her instruction "may not only be advantageous to this Hospital but an Act of Justice to the Girl." Although two of the boys had long and successful careers as church organists, Mercy's talent did not lead to a happy life. She eventually went insane, and ended up living in a madhouse run by someone named Dr. Perfect.

"Weakly" foundlings cost more money to raise than healthy ones. Wet nurses and foster families expected higher wages to care for them, and the governors also had to pay more to have them apprenticed. Tailors and shoe-makers occasionally accepted lame boys, as fitness was not necessary to do the

A lot more attention was paid to the foundlings' musical instruction than to their fashion sense. One girl in Hannah Brown's time was particularly admired for her ability to catch mice in her pinafore!

work, but apparently nobody wanted deformed girls, nor those considered "ideotical" or "deficient in understanding." These girls often continued to work at some job within the Hospital. For example, Ann Twigg was apprenticed twice and returned both times as unsatisfactory. The governors finally accepted her back to live in the Hospital, "employed in such work as she may be found capable of."

In the mid-1800s, a "Benevolent Fund for Adults" was established, through private donations, to provide annual pensions or weekly allowances to aged or infirm foundlings "who have been out in the world, whose laborious lives have been without reproach or whose sickness has been unprovoked by intemperance [excessive drinking] or other misconduct."

One foundling stayed at the Hospital, yet was very successful. He is first mentioned in the committee minutes in August 1814, when "until further notice, John Brownlow, No. 18607, [is to] be taken into the Secretary's office and employed therein." Three years later he was given a fine new suit of clothes and a salary of fifteen guineas per year. A year later, he was allowed to dine at the "officers' table."

Brownlow was promoted again and again, with a raise in salary each time. In November of 1828 he managed to extinguish a fire in the chapel store-room, and his salary was increased to a hundred guineas. He served as secretary for twenty-three years, and spent seventy-two years within the walls of the Hospital, first as a bachelor and later with his wife.

Brownlow was there during the time that Dickens wrote the novel *Oliver Twist*. It is surely more than coincidence that the great author named Oliver's kindly benefactor "John Brownlow."

It was at Brownlow's suggestion that the instrumental band was established, and he was also responsible for organizing the massive collection of archives that have preserved for us the history of the Foundling Hospital. His daughter, Emma Brownlow King, became an artist and painted several pictures revealing glimpses of life "inside," including some in this book.

John Brownlow was lucky to have a family. In their memoirs, many foundlings speak of the difficulty they had in falling in love and becoming parents. If a romance bloomed between ex-foundlings, they often decided not to marry because they would not be gaining the one thing they most missed: a complete family, with parents and uncles and aunts. Some felt unprepared for parenthood because they had no personal experience of what it meant to have parents; they had no role models for such an important job. For others, fortunately, "making a family" became the key to a happy life.

The Foundling Hospital cared for some 27,000 children during its 210 years. Almost all of them were white. Notes in the early records refer to an occasional "mulatto" (person of mixed race) and there is one reference to the baby of someone named Black Peggy, but these were clearly exceptions. So where were all the children of African and Asian descent? There were proportionately fewer people of colour living in London in the eighteenth and nineteenth centuries than there are now, but there must have been orphans and foundlings among them.

There is nearly nothing written down to tell us about this community. Parish records of births and baptisms don't usually mention race. Census records (not entirely reliable) show that black and Asian men far outnumbered the women; most of the men were sailors or slaves, or runaway slaves hoping to make a new life for themselves. (In 1772 it became law that "as soon as any slave sets his foot upon English territory he becomes free.")

Because there were so few women of colour, many of the marriages and partnerships – and the children – were interracial. It's not clear what happened to these babies if their parents could not care for them. Some orphanages must have had places for them. But the sad truth is that many children of mixed race probably died – or, perhaps worse, ended up in the workhouse.

CHAPTER SEVEN

The Later Years

n 1741, when the Foundling Hospital moved to Lamb's Conduit Fields, the area was rural and healthy. By 1926, London had expanded to surround it with noise and pollution. The governors decided that another move would be beneficial to everyone. The site was sold, the Hospital was torn down, and construction began on a new hospital, set in two hundred acres of land in Berkhamsted, in Hertfordshire. In the meantime, the children were moved to a temporary school in Redhill, in Surrey. The benefits of country living were immediately apparent. One foundling said, "Don't forget in London you had no grass to play on . . . but at Redhill we had all the grass and the trees. It was a beautiful place."

Nine years later, the children followed their marching band into a fine new hospital for the first time, and saw that it contained pieces of the original: the chapel pulpit, the stained-glass windows, and the oak staircase from the entrance hall. There was also a concert hall, a gymnasium and a swimming pool.

The body of Thomas Coram was there as well. It had arrived a few days earlier, to lie beneath the new children's chapel.

After 1945, at the end of the Second World War, there were many changes at the Foundling Hospital. An "after-care officer" was employed to guide

The Berkhamsted site, where the foundlings lived from 1938 until the Hospital closed in 1953. The cluster of cedars in front was called "the jungle," and the boys claimed there was no tree they couldn't climb. They also shinnied up and down the drainpipes, risking severe punishment if they were caught. This building, with the chapel standing at the front, is now a school called Ashlyn's.

departing young people into jobs or even college. Many of the boys continued to be well suited for army life. For the young men who had "graduated" directly into the First or Second World War, connecting to the real world afterwards must have been especially hard.

After the Second World War, residential care and schooling were slowly phased out for foundlings. The Hospital in Berkhamsted finally closed its doors in 1953, and the remaining children were given homes with foster families. The organization itself became the Thomas Coram Foundation for Children (and later the Coram Family). The buildings in Berkhamsted were converted into a regular day school, called the Thomas Coram School in honour of its history. The school is still open in 2005, but it has been renamed the Ashlyn's School.

The Coram Family – now housed in a building near the original site, next to the Foundling Museum, behind a public playground called Coram's Fields – continues to provide care in many ways. Children with special needs, and those who are HIV-positive, are placed in adoptive families who have been

Thomas Coram faced many obstacles in his life, but this good-hearted man's determination to help others saved the lives of thousands of children. He continues to have an impact even today, on the descendants of the foundlings, and on the children still cared for through the Coram Family organization.

trained to look after them. There are also specialist foster parents for troubled children who would otherwise be sent to reform schools. Since members of a family are sometimes forced to live apart when a parent is ill or in prison or rehabilitation, the Coram group offers a contact service to keep such families in touch. Nearly three hundred years after Thomas Coram went to his friends, hat in hand, determined to help children in need, help is still being given in his name.

What happened to all those children?

Hannah Brown's life was quite extraordinary. She worked as a domestic servant for fourteen unhappy years, in seventeen different jobs. She finally gave that up and became an artist's model, for eight years. She then trained and worked as a midwife, until she travelled and lived in Italy for six months, where she was inspired to become a painter. Her first exhibition (and her first sale of a painting, called *A Road in Tuscany*) was at a Royal Academy show in 1930. Her husband, Frank Brown, was also an artist. Hannah lived past her 106th birthday.

After leaving the Foundling Hospital, Charles Nalden joined His Majesty's Royal Artillery (Mounted) Band. He found the army barracks filthy and

A highlight in the year of the foundlings, from about 1905 to 1939, was a six-week interlude at summer camp, when the children were transported to the country to sleep in huge canvas tents, and trade in their heavy wool uniforms for lightweight khakis. Summer camp meant "freedom, better food, pocket money to buy small items in the village shops." (Apart from candy, some of the most popular purchases were salt and pepper!) The children slept on straw-filled mats, slid down grassy hills, picked wildflowers and had the chance to play with two or three friends at a time, instead of being herded in a crowd. And every Sunday they formed a parade, and marched to church behind their band.

crowded after the tidy Foundling dormitories. He went to a military music school and eventually settled on the French horn and the harp as his two main instruments. Charles stayed with the army for over twenty-five years, until he had an opportunity to become a music professor at the University of Auckland, in New Zealand. He believed passionately in the power of music to change lives, and was made a Commander of the Order of the British Empire (CBE) by the queen for his service to music. He and his wife, Peggy, had two children. Charles died in 2002, when he was ninety-four years old.

Ken Budden was claimed by his birth mother when he was fourteen years old. At first he thought this made him "one of the lucky ones," but his adjustment to that particular family's life was difficult. As soon as he was old enough, Ken signed up with the armed forces, and found that military life suited him better. When he left military service, he tried several jobs; he liked long-distance truck driving the best. He was married and had two children, got divorced, moved to Florida and got married again.

Although Ken is now retired, he volunteers as a school bus driver, and he admits that his foundling upbringing affects him to this day: he is very strict with the children during the ride, but he gives them all candy once a month, and they sing on their way to school.

As for my grandfather, John Graham Ranson, he was nine months old when his mother brought him to the Foundling on July 5, 1881. She must have prayed that he would have a better life than the one she expected for herself. There is no record that she ever visited him, or wrote a letter asking about him. Four days later, under his new name of Arthur Jocelyn, he was sent to live with a foster mother, Mary J. Taylor.

The British census taken in April 1881, shortly before Arthur's arrival, shows that the Taylor family lived in a village in Kent. Mary's husband, George, was a gardener. They had six children of their own: George, Eliza, Martha, William, Ann and Sarah, who was three years old.

Arthur was returned to the hospital on June 4, 1885, just before his fifth birthday. He must have been a healthy boy. There is only one mention of him in the matron's daily record, when he was among a group of children sent to the country for a few weeks to avoid a fever epidemic.

On November 14, 1895, Arthur, now fifteen years old, left the Foundling and enlisted "into the Band" of the Princes of Wales 2nd North Staffordshire Regiment. He played the clarinet and the saxophone. His discharge papers

Arthur did not stay long in Saskatchewan's farm country, but he did manage to form a band in Bulyea. Here he is, second from the right, with his clarinet.

show that during some twelve years in the army, Lance Corporal Arthur Jocelyn spent over six years "abroad." That time included service in South Africa, where the Boer War was raging, and a later stint in India.

Some time toward the end of his army years, back in England, Arthur went to a military dance and met a dark-haired young woman with bright brown eyes. Her name was Annie Pauline Bennett and she worked as a domestic servant. Annie had also grown up in an orphanage, but we don't (yet) know which one.

When Arthur was twenty-seven, in 1907, he left the army and responded to an advertisement calling for "homesteaders" to help settle the Canadian

Arthur Jocelyn with his new bride, Annie.

West. He made the long journey from England to Bulyea, Saskatchewan. After five or six years, though, he admitted that he was not cut out to be a prairie settler. He applied for a job with the Grand Trunk Railway and travelled east to Stratford, Ontario, where the main train shops were located.

Ever since leaving England, Arthur had faithfully corresponded with Annie Pauline. Now that he could expect a steady income working for the railway, he wrote again, asking her to join him in Canada and become his wife.

Annie Pauline bravely set sail for Canada to spend her life with a man she had not seen in eight years. The two were married on May 1, 1914, and their daughter Irene May was born almost exactly nine months later.

Meanwhile, the First World War had started in Europe. Though Arthur was thirty-five years old, he joined the Canadian Army Medical Corps, earned a massage licence and volunteered to return to England. Annie was pregnant again. Not wanting to be alone in a new country, she and Irene sailed back with Arthur, planning to live with friends from Annie's own days in an orphanage until the war ended.

Arthur and his wife, Annie, with Irene and their new baby, Mary.
Arthur is in army uniform; these are the dark days of the First World War.
The red cross on his sleeve shows that he is in the medical corps.

A second daughter, Mary Gladys, was born in London in 1917. Arthur served as a "batboy," or valet, to an officer. He accompanied him to France at the end of the war and was in Versailles when the Treaty of Versailles was signed in 1919, finally ending the bloody conflict. The Jocelyn family returned to Canada, and two years later my father, Gordon, was born.

Arthur's childhood in the Foundling Hospital clearly influenced his behaviour all of his life. Gordon and Irene both remember their father as a quiet, religious man who worked hard and attended church — a service, prayers or choir practice — at least three times a week. He insisted on saying a blessing before every meal, breakfast, lunch and supper; "a *long* grace," according to Irene. Perhaps, as he looked at the family dinner before him, he remembered those days of pottage and gruel.

Arthur passed along his musical heritage from the Foundling Hospital; he taught Irene to play both the clarinet and the saxophone. Mary played the violin and Gordon was a prize-winning pianist. Arthur and Annie often sang duets at church and community functions.

Arthur worked for the railroad all his life, until he retired at age sixty-five. Annie died three years later, in 1948. In his last years, Arthur travelled to England — and visited the Foundling Hospital.

One summer afternoon ten years after Annie died, while waiting to watch a Bible School concert featuring my sister and brother, Arthur himself had a heart attack and died.

An announcement was made inside the church that Arthur Jocelyn would not be attending the concert, as he had been "called home." *Home* — a word that must have had special meaning to him.

Glossary

(For kinds of clothing, see "Clothing," at end of glossary.)

Apothecary: early pharmacist, who also gave medical advice and made house calls.

Apprentice: someone bound to serve a master for a specified period of time, usually five or seven years, to learn a trade.

Cabin boy: a boy acting as servant to the officers of a ship.

Clyster: an injection or enema.

Debtor's prison: a jail where people owing money (and their families) lived until they could arrange to pay their debts.

Domestic servant: a house servant, such as a maid, butler or boot boy.

Dry nurse: a woman who cared for infants but was not a **Wet nurse**.

Foundling: a child who has been abandoned by its parents, left to be found and saved by strangers.

Gruel (or **milk porridge** or **milk pottage**): a thin blend of oatmeal, rice or other cereal stirred into boiling water or milk.

Guinea: a fashionable unit of currency; *see* **Pence**.

Illegitimate: born to parents who are not married to each other.

Inoculation: placement of a germ or virus into a person or animal, through a puncture, especially to prevent disease by creating immunity. *See* **Vaccination**.

Parliament: the national government, in Britain and many other countries.

Pence: British pennies, before the currency was changed to a decimal system; there were 12 pence in a shilling, 20 shillings in a pound and 21 shillings in a guinea.

Pottage: *see* **Gruel**.

Pound: the main unit of British currency; *see* **Pence**.

Privy: an outhouse or toilet.

Shilling: *see* **Pence**.

Smallpox: a very contagious disease, often fatal. People who survived smallpox usually had scars (pocks).

Vaccination: injecting people with cowpox (a mild disease) to prevent them from getting smallpox. (The word is sometimes used to mean any inoculation that prevents disease.)

Wet nurse: a woman other than the birth mother who nurses a baby from her breast. In order for her milk to be flowing, she has usually had a child of her own a few weeks or months earlier.

Workhouse: a place where poor people were given enough food and shelter to survive, but were forced to work in return. Workhouses were often filthy and crowded, and disease spread rapidly there.

Clothing

Barrow: a long, sleeveless garment for a baby.

Bays: baize; coarse woollen material with a long nap.

Bibb: bib.

Biggin: a muslin cap that bound the forehead tightly and was thought to promote the hardening of the soft skull of newborn infants.

Blucher boot (named for a Prussian field marshal): a short, heavy, lace-up boot of a particular construction.

Bodice coat: an undergarment for the upper part of the body, reinforced with whalebone stays, like a corset for babies.

Clout: diaper.

Froc: frock; a dress-like outer garment for a young child.

Linsey: a material made of wool and flax.

Long-stay: *see* **Stays**.

Mantle: a sleeveless garment, like a cloak but shorter.

Petticoat: slip.

Pilch: a triangular cloth worn over the diaper.

Rowlers (or Rollers): swaddling bands – narrow strips of cloth wrapped around a newborn infant's arms and legs to restrict movement.

Stays: a laced undergarment reinforced with strips of stiff material such as whalebone.

Upper-coat: an outer garment.

Waistcoat: vest.

Timeline

1668	Thomas Coram is born in Lyme Regis, England.
1687	Elizabeth Cellier approaches King James II to establish a foundling hospital that will also train midwives. She is unsuccessful.
1704	Thomas Coram returns to London after ten years in America.
1710	St. Paul's Cathedral is completed after 35 years of construction.
1722	Thomas Coram begins his campaign to establish a home for foundlings.
1727	George I dies. George II is crowned. His wife, Queen Caroline, is sympathetic to the plight of foundlings, and writes an article lauding L'Hôpital des Enfans-Trouvés in Paris. She dies before it is published.
1739	Thomas Coram obtains a royal charter from George II to establish a "Hospital for the Maintenance and Education of Exposed and Abandoned Children."
1740	Thomas Coram's wife, Eunice, dies.
1741	The Hospital is established, in temporary quarters in a house in Hatton Garden, in London. On March 25, the first foundlings are admitted.
1745	The foundlings move into the new Hospital – not quite completed – in Lamb's Conduit Fields.
1749	*Tom Jones, the History of a Foundling*, a novel by Henry Fielding, is published.
1750	On May 1, Handel's *Messiah* is first performed in the chapel of the Foundling Hospital.
1751	March 29, Thomas Coram dies. On April 3, he is buried in the chapel of the Foundling Hospital. The funeral is simple, featuring a single mourning coach and the choirs of St. Paul's Cathedral and Westminster Cathedral.
1753	The British Museum is founded.
1754	Hardwicke's Marriage Act is passed. Before this law was passed, people merely had to say vows in front of any witnesses to become lawfully wed. The Marriage Act insists that banns (prior notice) be posted and that the ceremony take place in a church.

1756–1760	The era of the "basket babies," or General Reception; the Hospital is forced to accept all foundlings under two months of age.
1759	George Frideric Handel faints during a rehearsal of the *Messiah*, and dies a week later.
1760	King George II dies. George III succeeds him.
1764	William Hogarth dies.
1767	The "Hanway Act" forces parish workhouses to keep careful accounts of incoming, outgoing and dead children.
1768	The Royal Academy of Arts is established.
1774	Oxygen is discovered.
1776	America declares its independence from Britain.
1792	Gaslight is invented.
1793	King Louis XVI of France is executed, following four years of revolution. France declares war on England.
1796	Vaccination is developed by Dr. Edward Jenner.
1800	The electric battery is invented.
1801	A resolution is passed stating that the principal object of the Foundling Hospital is to support illegitimate children, and the children of soldiers and sailors killed in the line of duty.
1803–1815	The Napoleonic Wars.
1807	The slave trade is abolished in England.
	"Troublesome" foundling boys begin being sent to the Marine Society for placement aboard ships.
1812–1815	*Grimm's Fairy Tales* are written.
1820	George III dies, and George IV is crowned.
1828	The London Zoo opens for scientific study.
1830	George IV dies without an heir; his brother William IV inherits the throne.
1831	London Bridge is completed after eight years of construction.
1833	Slavery is abolished throughout the British Empire.
1834	"Troublesome" foundling girls begin to be sent to Australia. A new law says that an illegitimate child cannot be cared for unless the parent is admitted to a workhouse.
1836	Birth and death registration begins in the United Kingdom.
1837	William IV dies and his 18-year-old niece, Victoria, becomes queen.
1838	The National Gallery opens in London.
	Oliver Twist, by Charles Dickens, is published. The novel features many orphans, foundlings and workhouse inmates.
1840	The first adhesive postage stamp – the Penny Black – is issued.
1847	An instrumental band for boys is established at the Foundling Hospital.
	Jane Eyre, by Charlotte Brontë, is published. The novel has several chapters set in Lowood Home, an orphanage.
1851	There are now more people in England living in the cities than in the countryside.

1861–1865	Civil war is fought in the United States.
1863	London's first underground railway opens.
1867	Canada becomes a nation.
1876	The telephone is invented.
1877	The first tennis tournament is played at Wimbledon.
1886	Coca-Cola is invented.
1889	Adolf Hitler is born. The Eiffel Tower is built.
1899	The Education Act makes school attendance compulsory for children under 12.
1901	Queen Victoria dies. She is succeeded by Edward VII.
1912	The *Titanic* sinks.
1910	Edward VII dies and George V becomes king.
1914–19189	The First World War is fought.
1918	Women over 30 get the vote in the United Kingdom.
1919	The T-shirt is invented.
1926	The Foundling Hospital property in Lamb's Conduit Fields is sold and the building is demolished. The school moves to a temporary location in Redhill, Surrey.
1928	Women over 21 get the vote in the United Kingdom. Penicillin is developed.
1931	The Empire State Building is completed.
1935	The Foundling Hospital moves to Berkhamsted, Hertfordshire. The London location is rebuilt to house the Foundation's headquarters, and the museum and archives.
1936	George V dies and Edward VIII briefly inherits the throne, abdicating the same year to his brother, George VI.
1938	The ballpoint pen is invented.
1939–1945	The Second World War rages.
1952	The Salk vaccine for polio is developed, but it will take another three years to be declared safe and effective.
	King George VI dies and Queen Elizabeth II assumes the throne. She is the eleventh British monarch to reign during the history of the Foundling Hospital.
1953	The Foundling Hospital is closed. Children still in care are put in permanent foster homes.

Source Notes

Publisher and date are given where a book is first referred to, unless the book is included in the Selected Bibliography. Extensive records from all governors' and Foundling Hospital committee meetings are now at the London Metropolitan Archives, and are frequently cited in *The History of the Foundling Hospital*, by R.H. Nichols and F.A. Wray, and *Coram's Children*, by Ruth McClure. It is these sources which contributed to this book. All quotes from Hannah Brown are from her memoir, *The Child She Bare*. All quotes from Charles Nalden are from his book, *Half and Half: Memoir of a Charity Brat*. Quotes from Ken Budden and Chava Cohen are taken directly from e-mail transcripts or telephone conversations with the author.

Abbreviations:
FH   Foundling Hospital
GC   General Committee, Foundling Hospital
LMA   London Metropolitan Archives
MHS   Massachusetts Historical Society

Chapter One: Castaway Children

The foundling numbers and descriptions come from the Record Book held at the LMA. Jonas Hanway mentioned "killing-nurses" in his essay "A Reply to C — A —, Author of the Candid Remarks on Mr. Hanway's Candid Historical Account of the Foundling Hospital," (London, 1760) "An Act for encouraging the Importation of Naval Stores from Her Majesty's Plantations in America" was passed in 1704 and can be found at the Public Records Office in London. The royal charter is on display at the Foundling Museum. The events of opening night are recorded in the GC minutes for March 1741. The quotes attributed to Dr. Brocklesby are from an anonymous essay published after Coram's death, generally believed to have been written by the doctor: "Private Virtue and Publick Spirit display'd in a Succinct Essay on the Character of Captain Thomas Coram" (London, 1751) Coram's letter about his wife was written on September 13, 1740, to his friend Dr. Benjamin Colman, who lived in Massachusetts, and is on file at the MHS. The report about Coram distributing gingerbread is from the notebook of Morris Lievesley, a long-time secretary at the Hospital (LMA). Reverend Smith's description of Coram is in a letter to Dr. Colman in January 1735 (MHS). The letter from Coram to King George II, written in 1735, is at the LMA.

The last paragraph, concerning the colonization of Nova Scotia, is from McClure, *Coram's Children.*

Chapter Two: Babies and Bookkeeping

The description of the "disgraceful scene" is from John Brownlow, *Memoranda; or Chronicles of the Foundling Hospital, including Memoirs of Captain Coram* (London, 1847), as are the account of how names were chosen, and the two quotes about Hogarth. Parliament's decision to end General Reception is in GC minutes for February 1760, as noted in Nichols & Wray, *The History of the Foundling Hospital.* The infant layette is outlined in GC minutes, cited in McClure, *Coram's Children.*

Chapter Three: Growing Up at the Foundling

The switch from wooden to iron bedsteads, part of a Health Measure of 1840, is cited in Nalden, *Half and Half,* as is the decision to ban visitors from the dormitory. The quote attributed to "Harvey" is from Oliver & Aggleton, *Coram's Children.* The quote "From the beginning . . ." is from McClure, *Coram's Children.* The recommendation about clothing and diet, and the recipe for plum pudding (noted in the Matron's report for October 1802), are from GC minutes, cited in Nichols & Wray, *The History of the Foundling Hospital.* The children's menus are from McClure, *Coram's Children,* and are on record, as is the governors' feast, at the LMA.

Chapter Four: Learning Lessons

A resolution against teaching writing was passed by the subcommittee in 1754, cited in McClure, *Coram's Children.* A 1757 advertisement for a schoolmistress outlined the qualities expected in foundling girls, cited in McClure, *Coram's Children.* McClure also mentions the library for boys and the need for girls to walk without "wadling." The note about adding military exercise is found in Nichols & Wray, *The History of the Foundling Hospital.* "Amy" and "John" are quoted in Oliver & Aggleton, *Coram's Children.* Coram's theory on the education of girls was written to Dr. Colman in 1739. Brownlow relates the story of the artists wearing foundling-made cloth in *Memoranda.* The agreement with Cuckney Mills, dated 1792, is in the LMA. The quote about mudlarks is from Richard Rowe, *Life in the London Streets,* 1881 (www.victorianlondon.org). The Andersen quote is from "The Little Match Girl."

Chapter Five: Illness and Other Woes

Dr. Cadogan's pamphlet is *An Essay Upon Nursing, and the Management of Children From their Birth to Three Years of Age* (London, 1753). Lady Mary Wortley Montagu's letter is from *Letters of the Right Honourable Lady My W — y M — e: Written during Her Travels in Europe, Asia and Africa . . .;* vol. 1 (Aix: Anthony Henricy, 1796). All quotes about health-related matters, as well as remedies, are from GC minutes, cited in Nichols & Wray, *The History of the Foundling Hospital.* The references to children of shame and the seamstress Quacker are from Brown, *The Child She Bare.* The comment about menstruation is made by "Helen" in Oliver & Aggleton, *Coram's Children,* also the source of the comment about having no excitement, made by "Ronald."

Chapter Six: Apprenticeship and Domestic Service

The quotes about abused apprentices, from court evidence, are cited in Nichols & Wray, *The History of the Foundling Hospital*, as are the sections about identifying the "Geniuses" of the children, and the words on Brownlow. The suggestion about Mercy Draper's instruction is from GC minutes, 1773. The quotes about deficient girls are from reports made by mistresses, cited in McClure, *Coram's Children*, as is the 1795 GC decision to keep Ann Twigg employed. The phrase from the Benevolent Fund is cited in the 1845 GC minutes.

Chapter Seven: The Later Years

The memories of summer camp are from Oliver & Aggleton, *Coram's Children*.

Selected Bibliography

Brown, Hannah. *The Child She Bare*. London: Headley, 1919 (?).

Brownlow, John. *The History and Objects of the Foundling Hospital*. London, 1865.

Dickens, Charles. "Received, a Blank Child," in *Household Words*. London, March 19, 1853.

Dickens, Charles, and Wilkie Collins. "No Thoroughfare," in *Christmas Stories*. London: Chapman and Hall, 1894.

Gavin, Jamilla. *Coram Boy*. London: Mammoth, 2000.

George, Mary Dorothy. *London Life in the XVIIIth Century*. London: Kegan Paul, Trench, Trubner & Co., 1930.

Harris, Rhian, and Robert Simon. *Enlightened Self-Interest: The Foundling Hospital and Hogarth*. London: Draig Publications, 1997.

McClure, Ruth. *Coram's Children: The London Foundling Hospital in the Eighteenth Century*. New Haven, CT: Yale University Press, 1981.

Nalden, Charles. *Half and Half: Memoir of a Charity Brat 1908-1989*. Wellington, NZ: Moana Press, 1990.

Nichols, R.H., and F.A. Wray. *The History of the Foundling Hospital*. London: Oxford University Press, 1935.

Nicholson, Benedict. *The Treasures of the Foundling Hospital*. Oxford: Clarendon Press, 1972.

Oliver, Christine, and Peter Aggleton. *Coram's Children: Growing Up in the Care of the Foundling Hospital 1900-1955* (a Coram Family Occasional Paper). London: Thomas Coram Research Unit, 2000.

Picard, Liza. *Dr. Johnson's London*. London: Weidenfeld & Nicholson, 2003.

Riding, Jacqueline. *"The Purest Benevolence": Handel and the Foundling Hospital*. London: Handel House Museum, no date.

Schwartz, Richard B. *Daily Life in Johnson's London*. Madison, WI: University of Wisconsin Press, 1983.

Tames, Richard. *Bloomsbury Past*. London: Historical Publications Ltd., 1993.

Wagner, Gillian. *Thomas Coram, Gent 1668-1751*. London: Boydell Press, 2004.

Picture Sources

Every reasonable effort has been made to trace the ownership of copyright materials. Any information allowing the publisher to correct a reference or credit in future will be welcomed.

For space reasons the following abbreviations have been used:

FM   The Foundling Museum, London, U.K.
LMA   London Metropolitan Archives, London, U.K.
PMJ   Property of Marthe Jocelyn, author

Page 1: courtesy of FM; 3: *Foundling Girls in the Chapel*, by Mrs. Sophia Anderson, courtesy of FM; 8: PMJ; **Chapter One** 11: *Panorama of London from the North* 1751, reproduced by permission of LMA; 12: *Gin Lane,* by William Hogarth, 1751, courtesy of FM; 15: *Captain Thomas Coram*, by William Hogarth, 1740, courtesy of FM; 17: courtesy of FM; 19: *The Admission of Children to the Hospital by Ballot*, engraving by Nathaniel Parr, after a drawing by Samuel Wade, published in the *Illustrated London News*, 1749; courtesy of FM; 21: *Statue of Coram*, by W. Calder Marshall, Royal Academy, courtesy of FM; **Chapter Two** 25: courtesy of FM, on file at the LMA; 26: all tokens are courtesy of FM, on file at the LMA; 27: Hospital foundling receipt, on file at the LMA; 28: Ordnance survey map, 1871, reproduced by permission of Guildhall Library, Corporation of London; 30: both pages displaying Arthur Jocelyn's records are from the LMA; 34: *The March of the Guards to Finchley*, by William Hogarth, 1749-50, courtesy of FM; 35: *Foundling Restored to Its Mother*, by Emma Brownlow King, 1858, courtesy of FM; 37: *Portrait of George Frideric Handel,* by Sir Godfrey Kneller, courtesy of FM; **Chapter Three** 39: courtesy of FM; 43: costume sketch by William Hogarth, and *A Foundling Girl* and *A Foundling Boy*, by Harold Copping, 1914, all courtesy of FM; 45: *The Christening*, by Emma Brownlow King, 1863, courtesy of FM; 49: *The Girls' Dining Room*, by John Sanders, 1773, courtesy of FM; 51: courtesy of FM, on file at the LMA; 53: *A Foundling Girl at Christmas Dinner*, by Emma Brownlow King, courtesy of FM; 54: *Sunday at the Foundling Hospital*, engraving by H. Townley Green, published in the *Illustrated London News*, 1872, courtesy of FM; **Chapter Four** 58: reproduced with permission of Peter Higginbotham; 61: courtesy of FM; 62: reproduced with permission of Hulton Deutsch Collection/CORBIS/MAGMA; 63: on file at the LMA; 66: detail of *The Thaw*, by M.

Acknowledgements

A book is never the work of just one person. In this case, my first effort at non-fiction, it was more than ever a work of collaboration.

It truly would not have been possible to write this book without the work of other writers before me. I appreciate the gracious permission from David Nalden and his sister, Rosemary, to quote from their father's fascinating memoir. I am also indebted to Ruth McClure for her remarkable book about Captain Coram. (We have made every effort to find Ms. McClure or her representatives and, sadly, have failed.) I treasure the unexpected friendship I found with Ken Budden, ex-foundling; his frank and funny memories of life at the Thomas Coram School were a tremendous gift.

I am deeply grateful to Gena K. Gorrell for her sure, guiding editorial hand. Thanks to my publisher, Kathy Lowinger, for giving me the chance to try something new, and for sharing London; and to Kathryn Cole, Kong Njo, Sue Tate and the rest of the Tundra staff for their unusual patience with me.

Other fountains of knowledge and assistance include Rhian Harris, director of the Foundling Museum, and the librarians at the Stratford Public Library and the Toronto Reference Library. Huge thanks to Aileen Hall, my fearless London-resident-on-call; she uncovered nuggets of information in many dusty corners.

For their various essential contributions, I would also like to thank Miriam Brown, Ray Marsden, Philip Swan, Jennifer Hubert Swan, Andrew McLaren, Linda Granfield, Gail Lord, Beth Lord, Sarah Knelman, Duncan Grewcock, Nancy Hawley, Edmund Govan, Chava Cohen, Phyllida Melling, and Joan Melling.

Special thanks to my father, Gordon, and my aunt, Rene, who were forthcoming in the face of my relentless badgering for memories and family secrets – and astounded by the result.

And thank you, as always, to Tom, Hannah and Nell, for hanging in there.

I am proud to acknowledge the Canada Council for supporting this project.

Index

The Foundling Museum

The Foundling Museum's remarkable collection of art and social history is housed in a historic building next to the original site of the Foundling Hospital. Although the Hospital building was demolished in 1926, its grounds – Coram's Fields – continue to be used as a children's park, where adults may enter only if accompanied by a child. The Museum and Coram's Fields next to it are located in London's historic Bloomsbury area, famous for the many writers and thinkers who have lived there over the centuries.

You can visit The Foundling Museum at 40 Brunswick Square in London, but if you can't make it to London you can also visit on the Internet, where you can learn more about the Foundling children through a selection of paintings. www.foundlingmuseum.org.uk

---

LORD Museum Books

LORD Museum Books are designed to help you experience museum stories to treasure from around the world. When you pick up a book, you make connections between the words, the pictures, and the story that unfolds as you read. When you visit a museum, you make connections too, connections between different kinds of objects from clothing, paintings, music, fossils, machines and whole buildings – to reveal a multitude of stories from real life. In many museums you can even get to listen, touch, smell and join in activities that help reveal the stories behind the objects.

A Home for Foundlings is based on the Foundling Museum in London, England. The Museum's job is to collect, preserve, and present objects and information so that we can all share in the stories of the past. Every museum has different stories to discover, depending on the objects it collects. What all museum objects have in common is that they are real things that help us to connect what happened in the past with how things work today. LORD Museum Books bring museums and the fascinating information they contain right to you so that you can enjoy them whenever you want, whether or not you have the chance to visit in person.
